Praise for *Get Clarity*

Success in basketball and business constantly challenge the leader or coach to develop a unity and commitment to getting the job done and a strong togetherness to make the team confident and powerful. Guiding talented people to have a strong inner game for themselves and their team is the key to success. Daily situations always challenge our inner game to shift thoughts and negative circumstances into positive energy and motivated possibilities.

The concepts and principles set forth in *Get Clarity* will help you become very clear about what you want—what lights you up. The Clarity tools will keep you vitally present and energetically focused on making it happen. Stay above the line! It works!

—George Karl, *NBA Coach*

The fusion of Cathy Hawk's brilliant *Get Clarity* methodology for facilitating personal transformation, with Gary Hawk's remarkable competence in developing the leadership capacity of CEOs and senior leaders, has given rise to this important new book. Don't pick up *Get Clarity* unless you are committed to revealing and connecting with your deepest calling. And if you pick it up, and you treat it seriously, watch out—your life will be SIGNIFICANTLY altered. Leaders steeped in Clarity will ignite extraordinary aliveness and effectiveness in employees in their organizations.

—Barry Heerman, Ph.D., Author
Noble Purpose, and *Building Team Spirit*

In these times of great challenges and opportunities, the need to lead others and ourselves with wholeheartedness, wisdom, and creativity has never been greater. The guidance system and journey map contained within *Get Clarity* will give you tools and strategies that will have you doing more of what you love and less of what you don't love. Whether you are leading a team of thousands, or a team of one, Cathy and Gary Hawk have laid out a powerful map to light the way. This book will get you there.

—Justine & Michael Toms, Co-founders
New Dimensions Media/Radio, Co-authors
*True Work: Doing What You Love and
Loving What You Do*

Get Clarity presents an extraordinary *Journey Map*. It is not often that a book provides tools, skills and practices that can guarantee clarity as its outcome.

—Angeles Arrien, PhD., Author
The Four-Fold Way and *The Second Half of Life*

The great knowledge, insight, and inspiration contained in *Get Clarity* are absolute gifts of the highest order.

—Janet Luhrs, Author
The Simple Living Guide and *Simple Loving*

What I learned from the *Get Clarity* process was how to rebuild my life from the inside out. It has changed everything—the way I view people; the way I see and do business; the way I view success and money; the way I view relationships. Every aspect of my life has been improved by Clarity. I originally thought something had to be broken to need this training. What I came to understand was that Clarity's program is especially for businesses and individuals who are performing well, and want to take their business and life to the next level.

—David Litchfield, CEO & Founder
Everything Good, Heber City, UT

The *Get Clarity* system gave me the confidence to launch and pursue my "lights," and exit the projects that no longer fell in line with my vision. I regard the *Get Clarity* program as one of the best investments I've made in myself.

—Feyzi Fatehi, CEO
Corent Technology, Inc., Laguna Nigel, CA

Thanks to the *Get Clarity* training that we experienced, our entire team has changed the way we work with each other and our clients. The increased focus and energy that our team has gained is priceless.

—Sue Goodin, Founding Director Progressive
Health Center, Denver, CO

Most of us may not be able to define good leadership. Some of us may have been fortunate enough to have either served under it or even exercised it ourselves. And, we all know it when we see it. In *Get Clarity*, Cathy and Gary Hawk have done an excellent job in defining the role of leadership today. The excellent example stories in this book help show us how we can use the *Clarity* approach and get better at it; even if we are only leading ourselves.

—Paul A. Riecks, President
Inner Circle Mid-Atlantic

Get Clarity

The Lights-On Guide to
Manifesting Success in Life and Work

by
Cathy Hawk and Gary Hawk

Books may be purchased by contacting the
publisher and authors at: *info@getclarity.com.*

Cover Design: Think2a
Interior Design: WESType Publishing Services, Inc.
Publisher: Get Clarity Press
Editors: Joan Duncan Oliver, Judith Briles and
       John Maling (EditingbyJohn)

Library of Congress Control Number: 2011929005
ISBN: 978-0-9835847-0-4

1. Business.   2. Change.   3. Mind-Body-Spirit.

First Edition   Printed in the United States

Contents

Gratitude

We are so grateful for all our teachers and guides, spiritual and human. And we remain grateful to all the leaders, seekers and lifelong learners who want to live vibrant, full lives every day.

Foreword

We first encountered Cathy Hawk in December 1998 in Sausalito, California when we personally experienced the Clarity method. Michael recalls being stunned seeing the "before" visuals of his face and then seeing the "after" visuals. The experience was so remarkable that he was catalyzed into a new cycle of his life.

He recalls Cathy asking him the question, "If you had all your druthers, with no obstacles of any kind, what would you do?" Spontaneously he replied, "I would travel anywhere in the world and talk to anyone I wanted to talk to."

Cathy then asked, "Who would be the first one you would go see?" Michael instantly replied, "His Holiness the Dalai Lama in Dharamsala, India."

Within four weeks of meeting Cathy and having this experience Michael received a phone call inviting both him and Justine to attend a special, invitation only, gathering with the Dalai Lama in Dharamsala. This eventually resulted in a private one-on-one interview with His Holiness in his home plus a great deal more.

Justine has had the good fortune of attending the *Get Clarity* training. This intensive retreat downloaded her with the tools necessary to move to the next level of pursuing her work with greater passion and skill. Cathy's river metaphor made a big impression on her. Justine says,

> When I could see the path mapped out like a river, I truly began to understand the flow of my creative endeavor. I could see the rushing river with the eddies, rapid runs, log jams, and even waterfalls.

This helped her to understand that passion and enthusiasm are a large part of the creative process; however, one must be vigilant like a river captain, skillfully rafting down the challenging rapids.

It is our experience that being aligned with one's purpose and direction is the energy that gets you into your river; however getting into the river is only the first part of the journey. Once you are in the flow, you need a clear map with simple and effective steps to assist you in finding answers, create breakthroughs and go into action to stay connected with your passion and vitality.

The guidance system contained within this book will help you answer such questions as: What's next? What can I do to get more vitality in my life? What is my purpose, my calling? When I feel lost, where do I go? As well as finding and following your lights-on flow, it will give you tools and strategies that will have you doing more of what you love and less of what you don't love.

Simply put, you have to continually ask the question, "What lights me up?" to get the accurate answers about your passion, and to know the next step on your journey. From our experience it's an exciting and lifelong learning process. This book will help you get there.

—Justine & Michael Toms, Co-founders,
New Dimensions World Broadcasting Network,
Co-authors, True Work—Doing What You Love
and Loving What You Do

PART I

Prepare for Departure

Introduction

To recharge themselves, individuals need to recognize the costs of energy-depleting behaviors and then take responsibility for changing them, regardless of the circumstances they're facing.
—Tony Schwartz, Author, Speaker and Consultant

Do you have *clarity amnesia*? Most people do at some point in their life: it seems to be part of the human condition. Sometime during your life you may have lost the awareness of your purpose and your passions. You lost sight of what gives you joy and energy every day. Yet somehow you have never lost a deep, innate knowing that it's critically important to wake up and know why you are here. What is your contribution to the world? How can you make a difference with your own unique expression?

No one wakes up in the morning saying, "Today, I am going to behave and act in ways that exhaust my energy, and I'm going to do whatever I can to drain the energy of everyone I come in contact with." Sounds absurd, doesn't it? And yet, that is the net effect of what happens day in and day out in homes and offices everywhere—people living and working with their energy and their enthusiasm drained and exhausted, having performed at less than optimal levels. This is an impact of *clarity amnesia*.

However, at some point, triggered by an illness, perhaps, or a loss or other personal crisis—even just a vague sense of dissatisfaction—something stirs within clarity amnesiacs. They become seekers on a journey to recover what they've forgotten. Clues appear; they can be baffled about which ones to follow. Then they begin to notice that following some clues seems to energize them, while following others exhausts them. As they pursue more of the energizing clues, their curiosity quickens. The process of remembering speeds up; they feel vibrant and alive. The spell of amnesia is broken, and a vision of how they want to live their life unfolds before them.

Nurturing that vision and taking it into action is what *Get Clarity* is about. It offers a guided remedy for *clarity amnesia*—a step-by-step solution to aimless wandering that will lead you on an accelerated journey to a fulfilling life of peak experiences.

Separately and together, we've spent almost forty years guiding people in aligning themselves with their purpose and direction. Even though many of our clients have come to us for help with something specific—discovering what's next in their lives, becoming a better leader, changing careers, perhaps, or finding their soul mate, we find as often as not they're in search of something larger and more enduring— living a lights-on life.

What does it mean to live *lights-on?*

- Lights-on living means that when you wake up in the morning you know you will be doing work you love.

- Lights-on living means that every day your relationships are vibrant, energetic and filled with grace and ease.

- Lights-on living means that you are conscious and aware—in every moment, of following your energy so you can live each day fully.

- Lights-on living means that you have the ability to see when your thoughts and behaviors are not working and to shift your attention to more effective ones. It's living with passion, purpose, and deeply connected action.

> Practically speaking, living lights-on means following your own energetic signals, moving toward what inspires and revitalizes you—what "lights you up"—and away from what drains and demoralizes you. Energy, in this sense, is the invisible force that animates life; some call it chi, ki, prana, or élan vital.

Although energy itself is invisible, its effect on the human system is obvious. Lights-on is a twinkle in the eye, a spring in the step, a glow around someone. Lights-off is equally apparent: dull eyes, drooping posture, a listless dragging through life. And you don't just live in your own, individual energy bubbles; you're part of a vibrating, pulsating, electric, energetic world—a biofield, a matrix of all the different energies of the people and natural forces around you.

One of our clients, Daniel, tells us that learning to live lights-on saved his marriage. Prior to learning how to read and follow energy, he had been frustrated with his wife, and for years had suffered a chronic discontent which took a toll on their relationship. He constantly thought of leaving. But with his focus always on that, he didn't focus on what made his marriage great. When he began to concentrate on what truly energized him, his perception of his marriage changed. Learning to discern *his own energy* is what saved his relationship, and his marriage.

Living lights-on means literally "going with the flow"—the energetic flow of the universe and your own life. It comes from honoring the process of life and the energetic feedback from your surroundings and your own physiology. Learning to discern whether people, places, or events are energizing or draining will quickly become second nature. We call this "cellular learning," because it happens at a visceral level: energy is experienced as a shift or feeling in the body. Your lights-on or lights-off response to daily happenings acts as an internal GPS—an energetic global positioning system to keep you on course living a life with clarity.

The *Get Clarity Visioning and Operating System* we teach our clients is grounded in making choices on an energetic level: taking apart the jigsaw puzzle of your life and seeing which pieces have energy in them—which light you up—then reassembling them in a configuration invested with more vibrancy and passion. A vision, as we define it, is that cluster of lights-on clues.

Get Clarity Journey Map

Our approach is action oriented: we use the image of sailing down a river as a metaphor for the journey to a lights-on life. For years, as Cathy worked with clients, the river image kept appearing to her as they talked about their life and their visioning process. She could visualize where a person was on the river and where he or she needed to go next. The image was so strong that eventually Cathy drew a rough sketch of a river on a long piece of paper stretched around the walls of her office, and marked on it the twists and turns, setbacks, and challenges that her clients encountered.

As she developed the *Get Clarity Journey Map*, it became clear that it represented a universal journey that all clients experienced. Clear patterns emerged, and clients began using the map to help them plot the next leg of their journey. With the map—and their energetic GPS for guidance—they could navigate rapids and ride out storms as readily as they sailed over calm waters.

> **When setting out on any journey, it is helpful to have a map leading you to your destination. The *Get Clarity Journey Map* is located in the back of this book, where you can simply unfold it, envisioning your own "lights-on" voyage. Both are designed to work together, with the stations along the river corresponding to concepts outlined in *Get Clarity* that can be referred to throughout your journey.**

How to Use This Book

Get Clarity is divided into five parts, each covering a different stage on the lights-on journey.

Part I: Preparing for Departure, introduces you to the visioning concept and outlines the fundamentals of energy, the foundation of our work. **Chapter One: Understanding Energy** explains energy fields and energy patterns in detail. **Chapter Two: Holding Your Own Energy Field** shows you how to retain you own energy under all circumstances—a critical step in staying aligned with your vision. **Chapter Three: Looking for Lights-On** gives you an understanding of how energy manifests itself in the human system. **Chapter Four: Using Your Whole Brain** highlights the effect your thoughts have on your physiology.

Part II: Setting Your Course covers the essential work of defining your vision and removing obstacles—internal and external—to moving toward it.

By **Part III: Casting Off,** you're no longer at your mooring, in preparation mode, but sailing in open water. Here you will experience the power of intention in creating reality; you will explore the push-pull of attraction and resistance in following guidance. You will also learn how to fine-tune your vision and align it with effective action, as well as how to navigate difficult choice points without being paralyzed with indecision.

Part IV: Correcting Course guides you through rough waters—the inevitable challenges and setbacks any visioning journey encounters. There is advice on recognizing when to push forward and when to drop anchor and stay still.

Part V: Sailing Home brings the visioning process to fruition, with Gary's story as inspiration. Here, you will discover the magic of synchronicity and the importance of living in the present moment. You will also learn when it's advisable to adopt a Plan B. You will get a taste of the "whoosh effect"—the exhilarating acceleration that occurs near the end of the vision journey, speeding you to your goal. We end with a recap of the inner transformation that signals a lights-on life.

In **Appendix 1—Peer Coaching** there are instructions on how to form a small feedback group of "strategic allies" to assist you in discovering and refining your vision. **Appendix 2—Get Clarity for Leaders** gives guidance on using *Get Clarity* principles to inspire a shared vision and create a lights-on culture in an organization. Since some of the terms we use in our work may be unfamiliar, we've also included a **Glossary** that supplements the definitions provided in the text.

Each chapter offers insights and strategies to reconnect you with your passion and true calling. At the end of each chapter are two summary sections to aid you in your journey. *Clarity in Action* contains real-life stories of people who have used these tools to create a new reality for themselves. In *Navigational Tools*, we suggest specific steps to help you move toward your goal. Taken together, the strategies and steps and personal stories in *Get Clarity* are designed to help you:

- discover what lights you up and what's next in your life;

- attract what you want and release what you don't want;

- create powerful relationships energetically;

- recognize choice points and use them to create your optimum reality;

- understand "shadow behavior" so it won't stop you from reaching your goal;

- eliminate self-criticism, judgment, and other debilitating patterns; and

- find the lessons—and silver lining—in detours and setbacks.

Our culture seems to endorse struggle and effort as the most effective means to achieve success. It continually reinforces messages like "Life is hard" and "Do it even if it kills you." But that is not the true path to success: diligence is one thing, but excessive stress and pressure lead only to exhaustion.

We propose an alternative—a "loving what you do and doing what you love" lifestyle. It begins with an inspired vision of what you want your life to look like, and then draws on your lights-on energy to achieve it. Passion and enthusiasm will help you create a vision. And having a clear vision to hold on to will keep you from getting knocked out of the game by others' well-intended opinions and advice, or your own doubts and fears.

The system and practices in the book are all time-tested by our workshops and individual coaching. We've found that people who've awakened to their destiny and are living a lights-on life invariably report the same thing: that regardless of the obstacles they encountered, they never lost sight of their vision. They simply adjusted their strategy, timing, or financing until they were able to see their dream come true.

In the pages that follow you'll find the tools and encouragement you need to overcome obstacles and complete your visioning journey, guided by the lights-on wisdom of your heart.

Chapter One
Understanding Energy

No doubt you can think of people you know
who seem to radiate stronger energy than others,
as if their energy field is somehow bigger or more potent.
—William Collinge, Author

As you prepare for your journey to a vision-and-passion-connected life, it is important that you understand your own energy and how it affects your thoughts and actions moment by moment. The primary tool for achieving your life's destiny is holding your personal energy field in a lights-on manner, in all circumstances.

You were born with a personal GPS, or inner guidance system—an instinctive knowing of what energizes you and what drains you. The concepts and tools set out in the following chapters are focused on helping you learn to use your personal GPS, so that you can control your own energy at all times. There are several important facts about energy that will help you in this regard:

- Your body is a biological energy field that interacts constantly with the environment, creating a feedback loop.

- If you interpret this feedback as stressful, the result will be a loss of your vital energy and you will feel negative, drained, and lights-off.

- If you interpret the feedback as exciting, the result will be an increase in your vital energy, and you will feel positive, energized, and lights-on.

Holding your own personal energy steadily and not letting yourself become drained or frenetic is the key to creating a vibrant life. To help maintain your positive energy in all that you do, recognize that there are three distinct energy fields that you are in touch with at all times.

The Three Energy Fields

Your Personal Field: The Human Energy System

Your personal energy field is the arm's-length space around you, like an invisible energy bubble. It contains your mind and your thoughts, your body, your health, your spirit and your creativity. You control your personal energy field through the moment-to-moment choices you make. By choosing what you think, how you nourish or deplete your body, how you exercise, and how you sleep, as well as how you enliven your spirit, you can stay energetically alive, conscious, and lights-on.

The language you use helps create your reality, so it's important to use positive talk and speak in a way that accurately describes the energy you are sensing in yourself and in the people, places, and situations around you. Avoid statements like:

> It *kills* me to hear that. or
> I'm so *angry* at /*afraid* of what's happening
> in the world.

The simple practice of speaking an energetic language—"that lights me up," or "that knocks my lights out"—will shift your focus, making you more aware of the energy around you, and will enable you to make better choices.

The Near Field:
The Environmental Energy System

The near field is the energy that your personal energy field interacts with daily, in your immediate environment—your home, your family, your neighborhood, your office, your community. The near

field is your support field. Although you have less
control over this field than over your personal energy field, your thoughts and actions have a strong
influence on it. You interact with your near field
constantly, so it is critical that you do all you can
to ensure that its impact on you is supportive and
enlivening. You can best affect this field in a positive
way by choosing your friends, partners, and immediate surroundings with intention and care.

To keep your personal energy alive in the near
field, ask yourself:

> Does my environment enhance my life?
> Do I feel soothed when I walk into my
> home or office?
> Do my friends, partners, and neighbors
> support me?

If the answer to any of these questions is no, take
the action necessary to change it, whether it's de-
cluttering your home, or letting go of friends who
are energy drains. (In later chapters, we'll suggest
specific action in this area.)

The Remote Field:
The Distant Energy System

The remote energy field is the one most distant from
you. This is the energy of systems and events in

the larger world over which you have little or no control—war, the economy, social upheaval, natural disasters. Even if you are not directly involved in these areas, you are impacted by their energy. From the time you were very young, the culture tended to direct your focus to events in the remote field. Think of the subjects you studied at school: history, geography, international relations, the social and physical sciences. The daily news bombards us with information about wars and conflicts, the ups and downs of the economy, crime, natural catastrophes, and global tragedies.

> **When you let negativity in this field consume you, and you worry about events you cannot control, you can easily lose your own energy, becoming anxious and on edge.**

To keep your energy alive when you relate to events in the remote field, reduce your exposure to the news media. Try going to bed without watching the late-night news, then notice if your sleep is more restful and you wake up with less anxiety. Listen to positive talk radio and other media outlets that deliver the news without using alarming language or voice tones. Tune in to positive messages and read publications that offer balanced coverage. This is not to suggest that you ignore what's going on in the world, but rather that you choose carefully how you receive the news, as a way to keep from being consumed by energy-draining negativity.

Calibrating Your Energy

Humans are hard-wired to look for light. Our earliest ancestors survived by quickly reading the energy signals of people and the environment. They would scan the horizon for areas of dark—signs of danger to be avoided—and areas of light, which indicated what was safe to approach. You still use this ancient communication system to answer the question, *Is there anything unsafe or wrong here?* In every new situation you automatically scan the environment to decide whether to approach or avoid. Once safety is assured, you move forward.

This same energetic scan ability is the skill you will use as your primary guide to making light-on choices for yourself. To make it easier to calibrate the energy in your personal field, we developed a simple tool—the energy meter—that allows you to assess the effect of your interactions on your vital life force—both external and internal. Any interaction with a person, place, or event generates an energy exchange. The energy meter enables you to guide your choices in the direction of more energy for yourself.

The meter registers three basic types of energetic exchange:

- Draining: You feel tired and worn out when the interaction is finished.

- Energizing: You feel more alive and awake when the interaction is finished.

- Neutral: The interaction has no impact on your energy.

Neutral

Lights-Off   **Lights-On**
Drained   **Energized**

At the low end of the meter, stagnant or lights-off energy is experienced as confusion, limits, mindless action, drama, and depleted energy. At the high end of the meter, lights-on energy, or "flow," is experienced as clarity, intentional action, a sense of possibility, and vibrant energy. Although it's arbitrary, in our experience, choices that calibrate at 7.5 and above are very clearly lights-on.

Using the energy meter as a mental reference point, you can gauge what will happen when your energy field comes into contact with other energy fields, so you can make choices that allow you to do more of what energizes you and less of what drains you.

Energy Patterns

Energy is an invisible force that can only be recognized by sensing or observing the effects or results of its presence. Energy in the human body is recognizable in the patterns that drive your behavior. To journey through life "in flow," you need to understand which energy patterns drain you and slow you down or stop you. Quickly recognizing energy patterns that are draining is what we call *rapid discovery;* using strategies to speedily return to energizing thoughts and actions is what we call *rapid recovery.*

Patterns are discernible in your own personal field and the fields of those around you. Just as a sailor uses knowledge of the constellations in the night sky to plot a course, recognizing the patterns in your personal field will make it easier for you to navigate while on your *Clarity* journey. Energy patterns tend to operate unconsciously; so to create flow in your life it is critical that you bring these patterns to conscious awareness. Of the many different energy patterns that exist, there are two that are especially useful to understand, because they have such a strong effect on the ability to live lights-on. These patterns are light and shadow, and *monkey mind.*

Light and Shadow

Light patterns are those that energize you and get you into flow, such as trust, self-esteem, generosity, innocence, curiosity, faith, vision, enthusiasm, cooperation, innovation, perfection, manifestation, playfulness, and service. *Shadow patterns* are energy patterns that stop you, such as fear, doubt, obligation, self-pity, anxiety, guilt, envy, competition, compromise, attachment, martyrdom, and imitation.

The more clarity you have about both your light and shadow patterns, the easier it will be to recognize when your shadow has stepped in to sabotage you. The shadow is always present. The psychiatrist Carl Jung wrote:

> Everyone carries a shadow, and the less it is embodied in the individual's conscious life, the blacker and denser it is.

Failure to recognize your "dark side" is a major block to realizing your full potential. However, when you focus on the light—on what energizes you—the shadow will lose its power.

People who successfully manifest their vision will first recognize their shadow behavior—that's rapid discovery. Then they are able to move past it by switching their focus and going into action with behavior that lights them up. That's rapid recovery. The premise is simple: if you follow your light you will *get* more light—you will *feel* more energized.

Monkey Mind

Monkey mind is a Buddhist concept that refers to the tendency of the mind to jump around like a drunken monkey, especially when you're trying to be calm. Put another way, monkey mind refers to the constant internal chattering in your head.

On the *Clarity* journey, we have a slightly different interpretation of monkey mind. To us, it's the critical, self-protective voice warning you of danger. In this sense, monkey mind has its origins in the fight-or-flight syndrome. This primitive alert system in the body interprets change of any sort as dangerous. The constant change in today's world sends a change-equals-danger signal to the adrenal system, putting the body on high alert. As the stress hormone cortisol builds up, it produces energy patterns of doubt, worry, anxiety, restlessness, fatigue, disturbed sleep, inability to focus, alienation, and hopelessness.

The most noticeable result of monkey mind chatter is that it distracts you from the present moment. Here's an example: Suppose you're lunching with a friend, engaged in a lights-on conversation. Your brain is interested and alert. Then all of a sudden, your monkey mind starts chattering about some trivial matter or judgment. While your friend is sharing something heartfelt, your monkey mind is criticizing the wardrobe choice of a woman across the room. You're still seated at the table, but you're not fully present. Monkey mind's internal monologue has taken charge of the situation.

After many hours of conversation with our coaching clients, we have observed some common patterns of expression that all monkey mind conversations seem to share. While this is not a scientific study, our observations are useful, and they add humor to a deeper understanding of this energy pattern.

- Monkey mind speaks constantly and is rarely quiet.

- Monkey mind has the speech sophistication and sentence structure of a five-year-old child.

- The monkey mind speech pattern is repetitive, saying the same things over and over, like a tape loop running incessantly in the brain.

- The content of monkey mind speech is overwhelmingly negative, laden with worst-case scenarios.

This constant din is a universal problem, and there are a number of meditative practices aimed at quieting the mind. However, even dedicated practitioners often have difficulty achieving a calm mental state for more than a few minutes at a time. So, if the pros find it hard to turn off monkey mind, how are we ordinary mortals supposed to override those tapes in our head?

Fortunately, we have found a way. Whenever our clients get stuck in monkey mind, we coach them to recognize and acknowledge the chatter, then shift their attention to what lights them up. The technique we use is simple: Instead of resisting monkey mind, address it directly by turning to your right and saying, "Thank you for sharing." Then, turn to your left and consciously switch your focus to a positive, lights-on action. You could, for example, do a check-in like the one described in the next chapter, or work with your vision map—a graphic presentation of your *Clarity* journey that you'll learn more about in Chapter Seven: *Designing Your Vision*.

Another effective recovery strategy is to find a relaxation practice that appeals to you enough to practice it regularly. Engage in some sort of mind-body practice, which can include prayer, yoga, deep breathing, and meditation to hypnosis, guided imagery, and labyrinth walking.

Chapter Two

Holding Your Own Energy Field

The antidote to exhaustion is not rest...
the antidote to exhaustion is wholeheartedness.
—David Whyte, Author and Poet

Life today exposes us to more drama—and melodrama—than ever before, especially in the media. It's easy to fall into the trap of confusing drama and energy. The key distinction between the two is that drama is draining, while energy is enlivening. To avoid being drained, focus on holding your own energy during all interactions. Learning how to consistently hold your own personal energy field is the most important element of creating the life you want to live. As you develop this critical skill, you will notice your personal field becoming steadier and stronger. With experience you will seldom feel drained, and the "energy vampires" will have to go elsewhere for their juice.

There are two key strategies to assist you in developing and sustaining—holding—a strong and intentional personal field—the *daily check-in* and the *daily personal ritual*.

Daily Check-In

The daily check-in is one of the most important tools to keep you in energetic and conscious flow. It consists of asking yourself a series of questions and paying attention to your answers. The time of day when you do your check-in is up to you, but if you do it first thing in the morning, you can start off the day with a clean slate. On the other hand, doing your check-in at night is a good way to clear away the residue of the day and set your intention for tomorrow.

You can do the check-in on your own, or with someone else. When done alone, the check-in is an internal conversation that will ground you and keep you focused. When done with another person, it becomes a very powerful relationship tool that deepens the connection between you and improves communication and understanding. But whether you do the check-in alone or with another person, remember that the primary purpose is to focus on yourself and on holding your own energy field against the pressures of your monkey mind and the energy drain from others in your near field. If you're doing the check-in with someone else, be sure to effectively listen to one another and refrain from commenting on or criticizing what the other person says.

The five questions to ask yourself in the daily check-in are:

- What's different?

- What worked and what didn't work?

- What is the state of my mind, body, and spirit?

- What am I grateful for?

- What is my intention for today?

What's different? One of the principles of quantum physics is that every nanosecond, everything changes. Noticing differences—what has changed, whether in your thinking or your surroundings—keeps you open to possibilities. Asking yourself, "What's different?" is a simple way to stay alert and avoid operating from old patterns.

The answer to "What's different?" doesn't have to be profound. Even a mundane answer like, "It's sunny today" or, "I'm tired" will shake you out of a world-weary, "same old, same old" mentality. The simple mechanism of asking the question helps you access a place of conscious awareness.

What worked and what didn't work? Review your performance over the past twenty-four hours, then ask yourself what worked and what didn't work. Comment only on your own performance, not on that of others, even if they were key players in the experience. This is very important. The intention of this part of the check-in is to remove all forms of judgment and criticism from your personal field.

This non-judgmental, facts-only evaluation of your performance is similar to what athletes do when they watch films of past games to see where they could improve. Be sure to give equal time to what worked and what didn't work. If you focus more on what didn't work, judgment and criticism are bound to creep in.

You're simply looking for information. Another way of asking what didn't work might be, "What in my thoughts and actions could I have done differently to be more effective?" If you begin to see patterns in what didn't work, you can develop strategies to change your performance. If you see that you frequently interrupt people, for example, you can set the intention to become more aware and stop that behavior.

Another step in this part of the daily check-in is to acknowledge your responses by clapping your hands to applaud yourself. This may seem trivial or silly, but it's very important to celebrate your answers, and celebrate them all equally. You're not really applauding the answers per se but rather your willingness to take an honest look at your performance and acknowledge what you discover.

What is the state of my mind, body, and spirit? The intention of this part of the check-in is for you to live in distinction—to be able to assess your energy and make choices from that perspective—by seeing a clear separation between your mind, body, and spirit. It is common to describe your personal field as if only one of those three areas was affected. For example, you might say to yourself, "I woke up with a backache, and now my whole day is ruined." However, a check-in might reveal that yes, your body aches, but your mind is busy and alert, and your spirit is light and energized. Hardly a prescription for a ruined day.

It's also important to note that your spirit is always described positively. Words like happy, joyful, expansive, light, soaring, calm, peaceful, and creative most aptly describe it.

What am I grateful for? Much has been written about the value of focusing on what's positive in your life. Research has shown that people who express gratitude on a frequent basis are more optimistic, feel better about their lives, are more energetic and alert, and make more progress towards their goals.

By answering "What am I grateful for?" each day, you shift your attention to what you *have*, rather than what you *don't* have. That focus allows you to approach your day with more vitality.

What is my intention for today? An intention is different from an affirmation. While an affirmation is a positive statement, such as "I am worthy of money," an intention focuses on action: "My intention today is to generate money flow, make six sales calls, and have fun doing it." The power of intention in achieving goals has been well documented. Manifesting what you want in your life begins with setting an intention, then taking action towards it.

Daily Personal Ritual

A personal ritual that you perform every day is the second essential tool for holding your energy. A ritual can ground you, connect you to your intentions, and anchor your approach to your daily interactions. When you use your personal ritual, you are choosing to live with clarity and compassion. The ritual can help you disengage from any drama in a situation, so that you become an observer rather than an absorber. Like a mirror you can simply reflect back the drama energy that comes at you, rather than soaking it up like a sponge. Your personal ritual sets your personal energy field.

Personal rituals can take many forms. We prefer a verbal ritual—an invocation that focuses on bringing positive energy into the personal field. You can create your own ritual by starting with the qualities you want in your personal field—peace, beauty, love, and the like. Make the ritual simple and easy to repeat either to yourself or aloud. Here is one example:

> *God, Universe, and all other Guides, grant me*
> *wisdom, skill, and knowledge to be of highest*
> *service to all. Assist me in holding a constant*
> *energy field around me at all times so that*
> *I feel only love and see only beauty. Let this force*
> *field attract others so I may attract love, joy,*
> *connection, community, and abundance.*

You may find it helpful to ground yourself before you begin your ritual. Close your eyes and visualize dropping an imaginary cord down to the center of the earth. With both feet firmly on the ground, breathe deeply and feel the connection you have with the earth.

If you wish, you can use a mudra or hand gesture. Mudra is a Sanskrit word meaning "seal" or "sign" that refers to the ritual hand gestures many yogis use during meditation practice. Other traditions also use hand gestures. For example, Christians put palms together while praying, and Qigong masters turn their palms to the heavens to call in universal energy. Any higher quality you aspire to can be sealed and activated with its own mudra.

It is very important that your daily ritual be done in a conscious manner.
Be aware of the words as you repeat them: feel them in your body; sense how they impact you. When you say, "I feel only love," or "I attract joy," let the feeling of love flow through your body and let the joy be expressed in your face, your smile. Most important, let your ritual serve you by reconnecting you to the sacred aspects of your life and setting your energy for the day.

As we've said, holding your own personal energy field is the most important step in achieving your destiny. The practice of performing a daily check-in and a daily personal ritual will help you stay aware, conscious, and focused on your vision.

Chapter Three
Looking for Lights-On

All that is in the heart is written in the face.
—African proverb

Looking for lights-on is a new way of seeing, and once you learn this skill, it will profoundly enhance all of your communications. Seeing what lights people up is an innovative approach to living that heightens your innate ability to tune in to the energetic signals and vitality cues that are constantly being sent and received. Learning to conduct a quick and accurate visual scan to identify levels of passion and energy in yourself and others is a fundamental skill for living energetically.

From the beginning, we have used camera feedback in our work so that our clients can see the physical changes that appear in their face as a result of focusing their thoughts and actions on the things that energize them. This photographic feedback is evidence of the power of their own energy, helping them deepen their understanding of what they can achieve.

> ⊚ **Lights-on is easy to see, once you get used to what we call high noticing—** reading energetic signals and vitality clues. When you light up, not only do you feel the energy in your body but your exterior physiology will also look different to others. High noticing applies whether you are seeing another person's physiology or seeing & sensing your own.

The following looking-for-lights tutorial consists of four pairs of photos, taken before and after an "energetic" interview—an interview that tracks a person's lights-on energy. The photos—each pair was taken in a professional setting under identical lighting conditions—demonstrate the physical transformation that occurred after the people discussed their most expansive visions with a coach for between 60 and 120 minutes. The differences in the before and after photos is striking. But even under ordinary conditions, you can see the same lights-on qualities in someone's face: balance, vitality, connection, and luminosity. In everyday interactions, people's faces shift rapidly, and your eye will notice the physiology changing from moment to moment.

In the first three pairs of photos, the physical changes were solely the result of a lights-on focus of thoughts. None of these people had yet taken any action toward fulfilling their lights-on dreams.

Increased light in eyes
Increased focus
More present and connected

Balanced light in both eyes
Right and left sides of
face balanced
More integrated overall

Increased focus and clarity
More present and energized
More relaxed and integrated

The following photos show what happens when lights-on thoughts are followed by aligned action. Here, six months elapsed between the before and after shots. They show the deeper, more sustainable physical change that comes with living lights-on.

 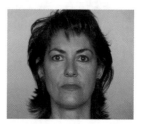

More luminosity overall
More approachable
More direct focus

Photographs used with the permission of the subjects

The changes you see in the preceding photos are a result of the body's ability to make an energetic shift internally, and then feedback those changes where they can be seen and felt externally. When you are tuned in to energetic clues and can communicate by responding to the energy of others, your interactions will be more vibrant and connected.

Pausing a moment to notice other's lights-on/lights-off energy is far more effective than living on autopilot. And calibrating your own energy by sensing your own lights-on level will enable you to redirect your focus and navigate choice points—dilemmas, transitions, log jams in the river—with certainty. You will have the power and knowledge to choose an energized future by following your lights.

Chapter Four
Using Your Whole Brain

Brain: an apparatus with which we think we think.
—Ambrose Bierce, Author

Your thoughts create your reality: *Change your thinking, change your life.* That sentence is a mantra for many of us, but what does it really mean? In the *Clarity* journey it also means that your thoughts can change your physiology; your cellular lights-on state; and your whole brain response. And that, in turn, changes your reality.

When you switch from a stressed-out, depleted, lights-off state to a calm, energized, lights-on state, it creates a sequence of physical changes in your system. You reflect, look, feel, act, and attract differently. Here's what we mean:

- *Reflect:* Lights-on energy emits a noticeable radiance and vitality—an inner glow. Lights-on is an inside job.

- *Look:* Lights-on energy has an overall balanced, lighter, more uplifted appearance.

- *Feel:* Lights-on energy is sensed as vital and timeless. It embodies flow with grace and ease. It is effortless.

- *Act:* Lights-on actions are purposeful and aligned with your vision. They're focused on doing more of what energizes you and less of what drains you. Before you act, you should ask the all-important questions: *What do I want right now? What will it take to make it happen?*

- *Attract:* Lights-on energy is attractive. The energy you send out is the energy you attract: Like attracts like. In high-energy exchanges, lights-on energy creates the magic.

What directions are you giving this vehicle, your body? Your answer is the essence of the *Clarity* journey. You are meant to live a balanced and energized life. And it all starts with your thoughts. Taking a vision into action requires whole brain thinking.

> ⊚ **Whole brain thinking creates systems and outcomes from a balanced communication between right brain (EQ— chaos) and left brain (IQ—order). Think of it as having a 360° awareness and meta-cognition. A whole brain flow pattern has the right and left hemispheres communicating and integrating information in a balanced fashion. The integration of these two dominant thought patterns lays the foundation for a balanced viewpoint which we define as global intelligence (GQ).**

Basic brain anatomy divides the brain into two symmetrical regions, a right hemisphere and a left hemisphere, connected by a thick bundle of some 300 million nerve fibers called the corpus callosum, which passes information between the hemispheres.

The right brain has been termed *emotional intelligence* (EQ). Dreaming, diffuse thinking or chaos works from this hemisphere of your brain. This hemisphere of the brain reasons holistically, uses metaphors, sees pictures simultaneously, recognizes patterns, and interprets emotions and nonverbal expressions. Well developed emotional intelligence is an accurate predictor of performance in a relationship setting.

The left brain is where *intelligence quotient* (IQ) resides. Linear thinking, planning and order work from this hemisphere. This hemisphere of the brain reasons logically, rarely uses metaphors, sees words in sequence, excels at analysis, and handles language. A well developed IQ is an accurate predictor of performance in an academic setting.

Here's how it works in your body. At the cellular level, when there is a balanced communication between the hemispheres, a cascade of hormonal events occurs and as you have seen in the previous chapter, the most noticeable effect is a radiance in the forehead and a twinkle in the eye, which we call lights-on.

This lights-on response to integrated brain functioning occurs at the site of the pineal gland which sits in the center of the brain, between the two hemispheres. Scientists now know that the pineal gland is sensitive to light from external sources like night and day. (A lack of external light is implicated in depression and seasonal attitudinal depression disorder.) The pineal gland is also sensitive to light from internal sources from the increase of or decrease of serotonin. For centuries ancient texts and mystical writings have called this pineal function a "third eye." This third eye response of lighting up reflects an integration of the two sides of the brain and it is associated with insight, or you might say, the mind's eye.

When global intelligence shows up in your physical body as lights-on, it sets the field for creative solutions and sustainable outcomes to be created. This whole brain way of thinking is an integrated communication system, a feedback loop. It is the key driver that keeps a vivid vision operating in concert with a strategic & tactical plan. The process then requires translation, through clear communication, into aligned systems and performance to make it a reality.

Using the skill of *high noticing* focuses your attention, and focused attention is the physical force which shapes the neural pathways of the brain. The lights-on response trains your brain to become the participatory observer—thus creating new neural pathways, which maintain and stabilize this learned brain state.

This *global intelligence* is a unified perceptual field of intelligence that is creative, insightful, and enables you to grasp the overall context that links component parts and binds them with meaning. This perception helps you to reframe your experience transforming your understanding of it, and create a *wisdom perspective*.

The *wisdom perspective* and resultant, newly created, neural pathways allow you to make more effective, high-value choices. When you communicate from a lights-on and balanced perspective, the translation results in coherent information. That information directs performance into an alignment with the whole perspective.

Review the qualities of EQ, IQ and GQ below:

Right hemisphere (EQ)	Left hemisphere (IQ)	Whole/global brain (GQ)
Movement on left side of body	Movement on right side of body	
Visual/spatial	Verbal	
Nonlinear	Linear	
Dreaming/what	Planning/how-to	Grasps overall context
Diffuse thinking/ chaos	Focal thinking/order	Cognitively reframes experience
Excels at intuition	Excels at analysis	Excels at linking component parts
Reasons simultaneously	Reasons sequentially	Binds component parts w/meaning
Sees patterns/ relationships	Sees sequence of concepts	Sees as an impartial observer
Sees pictures simultaneously	Sees words in orderly progression	Uses 360° seeing/ meta-awareness

PART II

Set Your Course

Chapter Five
Planning Your Journey

There is a vitality, a life-force, an energy, a quickening that is translated through you into action, and because there is only one of you in all of time, this expression is unique and if you block it, it will never exist through any medium and will be lost ...the world will not have it. It is not your business to determine how good it is, nor how valuable, nor how it compares with other expressions...it is your business to keep it yours, clearly and directly, to keep the channel open.
—Martha Graham, Dancer, Choreographer

Before we begin any journey—say, a long-planned vacation—we're filled with anticipation, excited at the prospect of having a wonderful adventure and open to the possibilities of what may happen. This juicy, energizing sense of anticipation is a wonderful part of the whole experience.

The same is true of the *Clarity* journey. Your enthusiasm for what you are beginning will generate the vital energy that will propel you to the next step of your journey. When you allow yourself to dream, and to be truly open to the possibilities for your life, you create a flow of energy throughout your body. You can feel it. And as you saw in the photos in Chapter Three, you look different, too. What's more, you act and attract in a different way. You are using your whole brain to create your vision and you know at the deepest level of your being that anything is possible.

One key aspect of starting your *Clarity* journey is giving yourself permission to have everything you want and to live each day vibrantly and passionately. Many people do not allow themselves the time and space to dream about what they want. As you begin your own search for what's next, you will discover that taking the time to experience your biggest and most passionate dreams will release a burst of energetic flow.

In a recent *Get Clarity* workshop we gave the participants a brief visioning exercise in which they shared with someone their dream for one small aspect of their life. In the discussion that ensued, one of the participants articulated a reaction we've heard many times:

> In just ten minutes of allowing myself to express what I truly want to another person, I felt more alive than I have in a very long

time. Merely talking about it gives me
incredible energy. I want to keep it going.

This burst of aliveness and energy is what we
want you to experience in this first stage of your
journey. Dreaming is a critical, energizing beginning
to putting a life-affirming vision into action.

What is a Vision?

Webster's dictionary defines a vision as "a mental
image; especially an imaginative contemplation."
For the purpose of your *Clarity* journey, a vision is a
collection of what we call lights-on clues—thoughts
about, and images of, a goal that deeply energizes
you when contemplating it. Your vision is a clear
mental image that creates a vital connection to unlimited possibilities for the future. Having a vivid
picture of how you want your life to be generates
energy at the core of your very being. As you develop
this picture in detail, it will keep you passionately and
relentlessly focused while you embark on making
it real.

Much has been written about what it takes to be
successful. One of the common denominators is that
successful people have a clear vision of what they
want to achieve and a passionate desire to accomplish it. In the *Clarity* journey, the vision we want
you to create for yourself is a heart-connected
image. A vision is more than just a good idea. It is a

good idea that is rooted in your heart, your passionate energy source.

Start Dreaming

To create a vision for your life that is driven by passionate energy, you have to exercise your right brain. Dreaming works from the right hemisphere. While the left brain is linear in processing information, the right brain is holistic. It sees the big picture; the left brain handles the details. The right brain is visual, dealing in images. Its mode of knowing is intuitive, while the logical left brain sticks to the facts.

Allowing yourself to dream, to imagine, and to be fully open to your intuition gives your right brain full rein to do its work. Many of the tools you will learn in this book are aimed at awakening and engaging your right brain. (Don't worry: there is plenty for your left brain to do on the journey: you'll need it for taking concrete action.)

Being aware of your energy and how it is impacted by your thoughts will help you engage your whole body in seeing, sensing, and using your energy to help you achieve your vision. So, dream big—let your most expansive vision guide you.

Clarity in Action: Ryan's Story

Ryan is a very successful cactus and plant grower. Before he was a teenager, he had a passion for the unique beauty of cactus and other succulents. Throughout high school and college his avocation was raising and mutating different variations of his plants.

Thirty years ago, after graduating with a PhD in Clinical Psychology, Ryan decided to take a year out before beginning a professional practice and spend the time doing what he loved most—growing cactus and succulents. He also truly loved working in partnership with his wife. His simple vision for the year was to be next to his wife every day, getting his hands dirty doing what he loved while creating an opportunity for others to appreciate having cacti in their home.

Ryan and his wife spent this first year growing cacti in their backyard and selling them out of his car trunk to nurseries in their area. As visions are prone to do, his grew into something else. Visions have a tendency to evolve and change when put into action. His initial vision led to a small leased acreage where he could expand his gardens, and expanded again to a vision of buying an even larger farm and significantly growing the operation.

Over time his vision became one of creating a much larger company selling varieties of cactus throughout the United States. Ryan's company now farms several hundred acres, employs a few hundred employees, and has revenue exceeding $70 million a year.

However, much of the original underlying and driving vision is still the same—working with his wife every day and getting cacti into homes so people can appreciate the beauty of the plants.

Clarity in Action: Sandra's Story

Anticipating a move to a new city with her husband, Sandra wanted to find the ideal house that would also contain her dance studio. To create an image of what she wanted she retreated to her meditation room, started dreaming, and began to develop an ideal picture of what the property would look like. What appeared to her was a house with a studio behind it. As she visualized the house, she began to experience what it would be like to walk across the patio tiles from the back door of the house to the studio.

The image was so strong that she could actually feel the heat of the tiles under her bare feet and the heat of the sun on her back. She could see herself walking from the house to a matching structure on the other side of the patio that had French doors and windows, and a skylight on the tiled roof.

Returning from her reverie, Sandra wrote down every detail of the image, including how she felt. Based on those notes, she created a visual collage made of photographs cut out of magazines.

With the picture of her ideal house and studio clearly in her mind, Sandra and her husband began exploring several neighborhoods in the city, paying attention to the energy they experienced in each locale. After finding the neighborhood that attracted them the most, Sandra began directing her husband where to turn and what street to drive down next. Her image was so clear in her mind that it was guiding her. On the third street they drove down, Sandra was astonished to see a home just like the one she had imagined.

What she hadn't envisioned was the landscaping: huge palm trees and lush foliage that created an oasis of coolness in the sultry climate. The other difference from her vision was the larger-than-expected listing price. However, the couple was determined to make an offer they could afford. After some negotiating, they were the proud owners of the home that Sandra had seen so clearly in her dreaming.

Navigational Tools: Start Dreaming

To begin the process of creating a vision, sit comfortably and allow a quiet space to open up in your mind. Imagine that you are somewhere that gives you a sense of calm, such as sitting by a country spring flowing with fresh, clear water. Plan to spend at least sixty minutes dreaming and exploring the place within you where anything and everything is possible.

- In this quiet place, begin to envision the changes you want in your life. Let go of any limiting beliefs or negative ideas you are holding onto. Be radical and expansive: admit all possibilities.

- Start by asking yourself this question: *In the field of all possibilities, what do I want?* (We call this the "Santa Claus question"—pretend that you're Santa Claus and can give yourself anything you want. What would that be?)

- After you have opened your vision to this unlimited place, you ask yourself:
  What do I want in my relationships?
  What do I want in my professional and work life?
  What do I want in my personal life?

- Stay in the vision place of what you want to create and don't get sidetracked into thinking about *how* you will make it happen. Trust that all action steps will come in right timing after your vision is clear.

- As you finish answering the questions and emerge from the dreaming state, be prepared to write down everything you remember— every detail of what you envisioned, no matter how wild or crazy it seems. These wild and crazy thoughts are what we call "lights-on clues." As you move forward on your journey, these clues will be combined with other clues, connecting to form a clear picture of your vision.

Refine Your Focus

When we are conducting visioning interviews with clients and ask them what they want, often the response is "I want everything." Unfortunately, wanting everything provides no clear direction, no specific action to achieve your desired outcome. To create a powerful vision that provides the necessary guidance, you will need to refine your focus by gathering more lights-on clues.

Cultivating curiosity is the first step to refining your focus. Being curious and exploratory about what you want opens you up to new ideas. And being aware of whether these new ideas energize or drain you will guide you in making sure that you are putting your attention on what lights you up.

> **Remember: Where you put your attention will refine your focus and ultimately create greater clarity. A clear focus will allow your initial dreamy vision to expand, and the resulting more expansive vision will show you in what direction to move.**

Remaining curious and paying attention to following your energy will also help you remain open to the unexpected. All kinds of wonderful mysteries and surprises await you on your journey, but if you think you already know everything, you will fail to notice them. The more you notice without the filter of your opinions and preconceptions, the more you will be shown. So stop analyzing and instead pay attention to what your energy and intuition are showing you. Refining your focus creates a refined, more expansive vision versus the aimless wandering that can come from wanting everything.

The bottom line in refining your vision is to follow what lights you up. Since your attention goes where your thoughts go and your attention directs your focus, it's critically important that you focus on what you want rather than what is not working. Focusing on what lights you up is a far more energizing, enjoyable and effective way to spend your days. When you operate on a daily basis doing what energizes you and serves a passion-based vision, you attract more of what you want. Like attracts like.

Take action by pursuing more of the lights-on items on your list. Doing more of what lights you up will naturally point you in the direction of your vision. And, when you begin to focus on the people and things that light you up, your energy will increase.

Clarity in Action: Bob's Story

Bob is an engineer working in upper management at a large mill in his hometown. He has always enjoyed the teamwork with his colleagues and the financial security and health benefits that the job provides. However, as the managerial load increased, it became harder and harder for Bob to feel excited about going to work. He felt drained, depressed, and trapped, but he couldn't see his way out of the dilemma of needing the salary from a job that no longer fulfilled him.

Bob and his wife, Karen, bought a cabin on a nearby lake for weekends, hoping that those retreats would re-energize him. Bob focused on being outdoors—hiking and river rafting in the summer, backcountry skiing in the winter. Soon he began to experiment with a vision by taking small groups of friends with him, acting as their informal guide.

Bob soon realized that these outings were his main source of enjoyment and fulfillment. He lived for the weekend and dreamed of turning his hobby into a full-time job. But the more he thought about it, it seemed like a fantasy that could never come true. He stopped focusing on the possibility and became depressed and sad.

Worried about Bob, Karen suggested he get some help. At her urging, he signed up for our extensive retreat, *Get Clarity for Life and Work.* When Bob was interviewed in the workshop, everyone could see that he was lights-on when he talked about being outdoors, acting as a guide, and taking people on wilderness adventures. Clearly, he was creating a deeply moving experience that enriched and transformed people. Guiding had started as a hobby for Bob, but the lights-on clues were leading him toward turning it into a business.

After the workshop, Bob decided to focus on developing the guide business and created an action plan. Looking at the big picture, he saw that he would need to stay in his salaried position for at least five more years, even though it was draining his energy. To compensate, he came up with ways to generate more energy in other areas of his life.

He began making plans to lead more organized, once-a-month adventures, and went about securing the necessary permits and updating his equipment. The friends who had already experienced the informal trips began to sign on, then friends of friends. Before long, Bob had all the people he could handle. He led twelve trips that first year, while staying at his regular job and continuing to receive a salary and benefits. As he began to focus on what lit him up, his depression lifted and his energy increased.

Bob is a perfect example of "what you focus on expands." Now, several years after his initial vision, he has turned his love of the outdoors into a viable, income-producing side business. Using vacation days from his fulltime job, he offers outdoor adventures to a growing roster of clients. All this came about once Bob stopped assuming that his dream was impossible and started focusing on what lit him up.

And once Bob began to pay attention to the interactions, thoughts, and activities that energized him, he developed a different perspective on his day job. He began to create a daily work schedule that focused more of his attention on the activities he enjoyed doing.

Navigational Tools: Refine Your Focus

Refining your focus involves identifying what lights you up. Be an energy detective in your own life.

- Take a 24-hour period, and throughout the day, be fully aware, and observe everything you do and everyone you interact with.

- Ask yourself two questions during every interaction or action:
  Am I more alive, more energized, more lights-on?
  Am I duller, more drained, more lights-off?

- Keep notes throughout the day on which interactions energize you and which ones drain you.

- At the end of the 24 hours, list all your actions and interactions during that time and rate each on a scale of 1 to 10 on the Energy Meter. Write down your ratings and note which items are lights-on. (Generally, anything above 7.5 is considered lights-on.)

Live in Distinction

Living in distinction means being able to assess your own energy by discerning whether it's lights-on or lights-off, then making choices from that perspective rather than out of habit. Making distinctions involves noticing changes in your personal energy field. You can practice it by pausing to reflect and asking yourself,

> *Where is my energy right now?*
> *Energetically what's different today?*

Noticing what's different or what has changed will direct you toward more energy and creativity. To make room in your life for more creativity, ask yourself,

> *Do I love where I am and what I'm doing?*

If the answer is no, recreate a new vision for what you want and be open to the possibility for change. Focusing on that question will rekindle the creative spark.

> **Living in distinction is a signal to do more of what you love and less of what you don't love.**

Learn to delegate the tasks you don't love. Being aware of others' energy as well as your own will help you discover someone who loves doing the work you don't enjoy. (Rest assured that as much as you *don't* light up about something, there is someone else who does!). Delegation frees your energy so that you can more readily make lights-on/lights-off distinctions as you go through the day.

Clarity in Action: David's Story

David, runs a very successful professional practice. As with many leaders who provide professional services, David was the CEO and the manager and he delivered the services to his patients. He loved working with clients, and he had a very clear and passionate vision for what he wanted to achieve.

However, the daily tasks of managing his practice exhausted him. He enjoyed relating with his employees and working with them as a team. However, he disliked creating and monitoring the systems, dealing with employee issues and supervising the marketing activities. Trying to be all things drained his energy, but he believed as a small business owner, he should do it all himself. He had been doing it for years and was financially successful. Unfortunately, he was often exhausted and irritable at the end of the day.

When he created his vision of an ideal day, he realized that 75 percent of the activities he was currently trying to do were not on the list. And yet, they obviously needed to be done to have a successful, vibrant practice. David realized he needed a manager other than himself to take his vision and translate it into a daily reality. He needed someone who loved building systems and developing and managing people so he could devote his time and energy to doing what he loved most—patient care and holding the big vision for his practice.

Taking the time to reflect on his vision for his ideal day gave David the insight necessary for him to hire a manager and delegate the tasks that drained his energy to someone who loved doing them. As a result, his practice has grown exponentially; he's far more energized every day and able to keep his vision alive and vibrant.

All things are possible; the only limitations are the ones that you place upon yourself. Limitless, multiple choice thinking creates an energy field full of possibilities. It forms when you fill yourself up versus depleting yourself. If you feel yourself going lights-off or losing energy, immediately stop and ask yourself the Santa Claus question: If I can have anything I want right now, what will that look like? Answer as if anything is possible—be both specific and expansive.

Clarity in Action: Sharon's Story

Sharon, a successful graphic designer and entrepreneur who runs her own business, realized that even though she was doing work she loved, she was becoming drained. She was focusing more on holding on to her energy than she was on being creative.

Sharon noted the differences in her energy levels when she shifted her focus from patterns and routines that drained her toward tasks that lit her up. Through this method she was able to discern quickly what parts of her work she wanted to continue doing and what parts she needed help with.

She began her analysis by looking at the overall flow pattern of a normal day. Sharon would start by meeting with a client to determine the requirements for their project then return to her studio to create five or six preliminary designs. She would then revisit the client with the sample designs to see what appealed and discuss any changes. After that, she would go back to the studio a second time to make the revisions, create a final design, and draw up an estimate.

Sharon asked herself, *Do I love where I am and what I'm doing?* She saw that there were two main aspects of her work that brought her joy: the freedom of being her own boss, and creating beautiful graphic pieces for her clients. All the scheduling and the back-and-forth travel to client meetings were tiring her and taking hours away from her design work. Being by herself in the quiet of her studio, immersed in the creative process, was what lit her up.

However, the other business processes were critical and still had to be done—just not by Sharon herself. As she became clear about which tasks drained her, she was able to write a job description that included everything on her lights-off list. Still, she hesitated to hire someone for the job, assuming that if she didn't like a certain task, neither would anyone else. But despite these misgivings, she persevered and found Maggie. Maggie loved the idea of meeting with clients to present the preliminary designs, then coaching them through the choice process and feeding the information back to Sharon.

From the beginning, Sharon and Maggie worked so well together that they decided to form a business partnership. Since then they've expanded, becoming one of the top design firms in their city—a success neither could have achieved on her own. Using the *Clarity* process, Sharon went from working alone and lights-off to working lights-on with a partner. Two years into their partnership, Sharon and Maggie realized that neither of them was lights-on about accounting, so they hired someone for that position. Now, the design process, client meetings, and financial functions are all being handled by people who love what they do.

Navigation Tools: Your Ideal Day

David and Sharon used the Ideal Day exercise to help them figure out which activities were lights-on for them and which were energy drains. With the list of lights-on clues you identified in the "Refine Your Focus" exercise to guide you, write a description of your Ideal Day.

- Where are you living and working?

- What time do you get up and go to bed?

- What do you feel like?

- Who is with you, or helping you?

- Who is on your team, both at home and at work?

Scan your personal and near fields using the Energy Meter. Note everything that registers 7 or above and include these elements in your vision of your Ideal Day. Add anything else that gives you lights-on energy.

Now go back and look for any people, places, activities, or situations that are draining your energy. Make a lights-off task list to help you delegate the things that drain you.

Chapter Six

Practicing Sacred Selfishness

Sacred (s / kr d) adj. worthy of respect; venerable
—The American Heritage Dictionary

This is the perfect place in your process of energy detecting to gain clarity about what you really want in your life, separate from the wants and needs of others. What you discover here will be pivotal in designing your vision, ensuring that your needs are met and that you have a reserve of time, money, love, joy, vitality, and creativity to use as generously as you wish.

We call this notion *sacred selfishness*. To function fully and effectively, you must serve yourself, and your vision, before serving others. It is like those in-flight emergency instructions that tell you to put on your own oxygen mask before you try to help other passengers with theirs, so that you both stay alive. You cannot give to others if your personal energy field is drained and you are an empty vessel. Being a martyr serves no one. Cultivating *sacred selfishness* is an important part of learning how to hold your own energy field and preserve your vitality.

When you hold your own energy field in a lights-on manner, you feel full and content, and able to be generous. It seems paradoxical to link selfishness and generosity, yet in the context of using your energy mindfully, it makes perfect sense.

If you feel yourself going lights-off—losing energy—immediately stop and ask yourself "the Santa Claus question": **If I could have anything I wanted, what would that be?** Remember to answer as if anything is possible: be very specific even as you open your mind to all possibilities. Expansive thinking creates an energy field that is free of limitation.

Clarity in Action: Riley's Story

When Riley entered the *Get Clarity* retreat, she owned a very successful real estate marketing business. Her firm managed the entire sales process for developers as they created and built new housing projects. She gave the developers design ideas that would appeal to buyers, created all the sales and marketing materials, and hired and managed the entire sales team.

Riley really loved this initial phase of launching a new project. However, she began to notice that even with a lot of staff to help her, she was running herself ragged. In addition to work she loved, she had a philanthropic passion: she was in charge of an international non-profit relief project to help refugees. Riley was going in so many different directions that she felt scattered and ungrounded and couldn't decide what was really important to her. Basically, everything she was doing lit her up, but it also exhausted her.

In a coaching session, Riley reviewed her daily schedule and assigned each task a rating on the Energy Meter. All of her daily tasks lit her up at 7 or above, so she had to make an even finer distinction and rate her tasks by "big lights"—9 or above. This process helped her distinguish what was most important to her, enabling her to focus her energy and attention.

When Riley was asked the Santa Claus question, she began sorting through all her daily activities. It was important for her to notice that whenever she felt drained by one of her projects, the project itself was also experiencing an energy drain. Her energy level had a ripple effect on everything around her. When she filled herself with energy, a field of possibility and generosity opened up.

Using the principle of sacred selfishness, Riley distilled her commitments down to the two she loved most: being the visionary for her real estate business and the visionary for the overseas relief project. It also became clear what was draining her: continually running around raising funds and performing administrative errands. She hired a detail person for each of her projects so she could delegate those tasks.

Shifting from being a "control freak" to a "control tower" enabled Riley to perform her lights-on role as the visionary. And now, because of her clarity and delegation, both projects have doubled in effectiveness and capacity. Being very clear about what she wanted—her vision—before figuring out how to accomplish it conserved Riley's energy for getting the job done.

Navigational Tools: The Santa Claus Question

The Santa Claus Question is one of our most effective tools for figuring out what you want. But often people find it hard to answer honestly: they don't feel deserving enough to dream big. To assist you in thinking expansively, enlist the help of a friend. Pick someone who promises not to comment on or give opinions about your answers. Your friend's job will be to ask you, "If I were Santa Claus and could give you anything you wanted, what would that be?" repeating the question until you run out of answers.

- Take time to explore each of your responses to the questions so that you get a true reading of your energy.

- Ignore the "how-to." This is key. If you go to the *how-to*—the strategy and tactics for achieving your vision—before you have clearly defined the *what*—you will deplete your energy and block the flow of the visioning process.

- Ask your friend to be a scribe and write down *only* your lights-on answers. If you catch yourself talking about what you *don't* want, go back and state only what you do want. Make sure that your scribe writes down all your lights-on responses even if they seem random and disconnected from each other. You may discover that some seemingly random thought opens the door to a new energetic perspective on whatever you are envisioning.

Another discovery process that many people find helpful is forming a feedback team we call *Peer Coaching*. This is a very valuable exercise that provides energetic feedback so you can gain more information on what lights you up. Plus, *Peer Coaching* expands your team of strategic allies—mutually supportive partners in creating envisioned lives. (For instructions on setting up and working with a *Peer Coaching* feedback group, see Appendix.)

Chapter Seven
Designing Your Vision

When master sculptors make figures out of wood or stone,
they do not introduce the figure into the wood,
but chisel away the fragments that concealed the figure;
they give nothing to the wood, rather they take
away from it, letting fall beneath the chisel the outer layers,
removing the rough covering, and then what
had lain hidden beneath shines out
—Meister Eckhart, Theologian and Christian Mystic

Designing your vision is the next step in preparing to move into the energetic flow of your journey. You are building on the clues you've been gathering by noticing what you want to take with you—whatever is lights-on—and the lights-off elements you want to leave behind.

Basically, you are beginning to load your cargo onto your metaphorical sailboat and building the navigation system that will guide it. Your cargo is composed of the people, situations, activities, objects, and thoughts that energetically serve your vision. The navigation system consists of your lights-on and lights-off responses to your cargo. It will steer you through the necessary course corrections as you move into the flow of the river.

The skill of tuning in to energetic signals and vitality clues in yourself and the environment is what we call *high noticing*. Your near field, which includes the people around you and your physical surroundings, mirrors the energetic signals you are sending and receiving. Your outer world reflects your inner state, in other words. If you feel confusion coming from the near field, there may be some form of confusion and internal clutter in your thoughts. Conversely, if you feel clear, then a feeling of clarity will be reflected back to you by your surroundings.

Clarity in Action: Virginia's Story

Virginia worked in a division of a large international company. Eight years of sitting at a desk and working on a computer had resulted in physical stress: stiffness, joint pain, and neck aches. She enjoyed her work but realized that her body was signaling that she was ready for a change.

She became interested in the exercise system known as Pilates. She hired a personal Pilates trainer and started exercising two days a week. Almost instantly she noticed big differences: the pain and stiffness in her body eased, and she was more comfortable. And while she was exercising, she experienced a very pleasant sense of timelessness. She would look at her watch and be surprised to see that hours had gone by. Paying close attention to all the energetic shifts within herself, Virginia soon became clear that she wanted to practice Pilates full time, as an instructor. What had started as a simple health regime had provided a lights-on clue to a new career.

Virginia began volunteering at a friend's Pilates studio several evenings a week. She discovered that while she was in the studio, she was lights-on, and wondered what it would be like to stop working in the corporate world, become certified as a Pilates instructor, and open her own exercise studio. Would she enjoy being an entrepreneur, or would turning her hobby into a business "knock her lights out"?

She continued to pay high attention to her energy both in her day job and in the studio. As she became clear about her passion for her new work, her confusion dissipated, and she could see that her next step was to sign up for Pilates instructor training.

Realizing that it would take about a year to make the transition, Virginia began designing her vision by creating a plan. She would keep her day job so she would have financial security, then focus the rest of her time, money, and energy on her new vision. Her plan allowed time to complete the teacher training and become certified, and to design her studio, purchase needed equipment, and line up clients.

Two years after she created her vision and put her plan into action, Virginia quit her job and opened a studio that was already fully booked with clients. Today, she and her business are thriving, as she continues to live her vision.

Clearing Clutter

Designing a vision is as much about removing obstacles to realizing your dream as it is about having the dream in the first place. Your outer surroundings reflect your inner state, and sometimes you can't see your vision clearly until you've cleared away clutter—anything in your personal field or near field that drains your energy and stops you from moving forward. Sometimes what prevents you from going into flow is, quite literally, physical clutter.

For some people, one of the most important steps in designing a vision is rolling up their sleeves and cleaning house. If this sounds familiar, your task is to identify and remove all the accumulated stuff in your home and/or office that doesn't light you up. For our client, Arlene, clearing clutter and simplifying her life made all the difference in creating flow.

Creating in Action: Arlene's Story

Arlene wanted a new vision and new changes in her life when she began the *Clarity* process. She lived in a large home filled with many beautiful objects—collections with meaning and value to her. She had a home office that was filled with files and paperwork from her business. A second office, outside her home, where she met clients, was stuffed with paper, files, and business equipment. On top of that, she had a weekend beach house.

The realization that her collections felt like too much "stuff" was a big clue to what was draining Arlene's energy and blocking her ability to move forward with ease and clarity. With her possessions spread over three different locations, she spent a lot of time searching for things. This unproductive and aimless use of her time drained her, and she felt scattered and unable to decide what she wanted to do next. It became clear to Arlene that clutter was creating her confusion and lack of flow.

Her first step was to begin clearing the clutter. She spent time in each location noting everything that calibrated at less than 7.5 on the Energy Meter. As she walked through her outside office, Arlene noticed that the space itself did not light her up; on the contrary, it drained her energy. She decided to downsize into one office space. That task seemed so overwhelming, however, that she hired a professional organizer to help her sort, systematize, and consolidate everything into her home office. Once she was able to find things more easily, Arlene began to feel clear, focused, and energized.

A year later, Arlene realized that traveling between her main house and the beach house wasn't lighting her up anymore. She decided to sell the beach house and again brought in the professional organizer to help her downsize. She saved only the things that she really loved from the beach house and brought them back to her main house.

Over time, Arlene realized that she still felt overwhelmed by her possessions, so she embarked on yet another clearing process. It took about a year to sort through and consolidate her belongings and clear out what she didn't want. When it was done, Arlene noticed that she felt very clear and fully present. She could walk into her home—and home office—and be focused, directed, and ready for business.

Now both her life and business have flow. Arlene lives and works with clarity and ease, surrounded only by things that light her up.

Navigational Tools: Designing Your Vision

Designing a vision is a step-by-step process incorporating all the tools you've learned so far. Practice *high noticing* and *clear clutter* to eliminate anything that does not support or facilitate your vision, then use the Ideal Day exercise to gather lights-on clues for making a Vision Map.

Practice High Noticing:

- Pay close attention to what shows up in your personal and near fields. See where there is clarity and where there is confusion.

- List the things that energize you and create clarity, and those that drain you and create confusion.

Clear Away Clutter:

- Scan your personal and near fields with the Energy Meter. Remove anything that registers lights-off or create a strategy for dealing with it that will bring you lights-on energy.

Experience Your Ideal Day:

- Using the description of your Ideal Day from the Chapter Five, *Navigational Tools*, do everything you listed in the exercise.

- Pay attention to where your thoughts are; what energetic flow you are feeling; what is happening in your near field.

- Be aware of additional clues that may show up during the day.

- Write down your experiences in your journal, and add any new lights-on clues to your vision list.

Create a Vision Map:

- Review all the lights-on clues you have discovered so far and create a Vision Map— a visual image of what you want to create in your life. Don't worry if you are not an artist; many people cut images out of magazines and paste them onto paper or poster board.

- The form is not important: you are simply putting together images that speak to the essence of your vision. Expressing your dreams graphically or pictorially taps into the qualities of the right brain, allowing you to connect to your vision in a deeper way.

- Place your map in a prominent place so you can see it often. Having a visual representation of your vision will keep you focused and energized as you cast off on your journey.

PART III

Cast Off

Chapter Eight

Choosing Intention, Creating Attraction

Let yourself be silently drawn by the stronger pull
of what you really love.
—Jalal-Uddin Rumi, Turkish Sufi Mystic Poet

You are now casting off with a deep understanding of where you want to go. You have assembled your lights-on clues and created your Vision Map. You are clear on your direction and what you want to create. Guided by this vision, you must now be intentional in everything you do. When you are intentional in your thoughts, words, and actions, you send out energy that will attract to you the people, situations, and material support that you need to reach your goal.

An intention is a strong purpose or vision driven by effective action and direction. Being intentional is a vital aspect of the *Clarity* process. It builds a co-creative field of energy with the divine in which all things are possible. Every aspect of your life is positively impacted when you approach it with conscious intention. A heart-connected vision, coupled with an intention, shifts your attention to the actions and behaviors that lead to a realized life.

It is easy to fall into the trap of living unconsciously. But getting clarity requires you to be fully conscious—present and aware of all your thoughts and actions. Choosing intention is one of the most powerful methods for achieving your vision. Clear intentions equal clear results. When you set your intentions every day, you will cease to be an accidental tourist on your life's journey.

Clarity in Action: James' Story

A member of one of Gary's business owner peer groups was founder of a small manufacturing company in Southern California. In ten years James had built the company from a garage operation to over $4 million in sales. For several months he had been lamenting the difficulty he was having with his production.

He couldn't find experienced employees; his production manager created dissension in the plant instead of cooperation, but he was afraid to fire him or even have a corrective conversation with him in fear he would quit. He actually felt that it was better to have an ineffective manager than no manager at all.

James was totally focused on the impossibility of finding a quality manager. He said several times that it was literally impossible to find experienced people in his industry unless he brought in someone from Europe. During a meeting, Gary was describing to the group how he had used a manifestation formula to find and meet Cathy. James wondered if he could apply this process to his need for a more effective manager.

He gave it a try. To set his intention he made a list of all the characteristics he wanted in a production manager and began to put his attention to finding that person. Most of his focus was on trying to find a way to bring an experienced person from Europe. To do this required sorting through immigration restrictions; this was not an easy obstacle to overcome. Through his European contacts he began to strategize how he would meet and persuade someone to move to his little company in California.

And then serendipity stepped in, as it is wont to do when the intention is clear. While visiting a facility in Mexico, James observed a plant manager who impressed him with his ability to build relationships with his employees.

This man had many years of successful experience in a somewhat similar facility; however, he did not have a college degree and he wasn't familiar with the technology James used in his plant. James' original intention was to find a good manager who also really understood the machinery. That's why he was focused on going to Europe where the machines were manufactured.

Ultimately, James decided to let go of his determination that he needed tightly defined requirements. He hired the man without all the technical experience. What he got as a result of his intention was someone who really knew how to build relationships, trust and a desire to do good work. Within a couple of months, James told us that the new manager was an incredible addition to his team. Production was up and James could focus on what he really wanted to do each day.

When you are clear with your thoughts, actions and words, you will always send out attractive energy. This will always attract what you need, if not always exactly as you expected.

As humans, we want to know all the details. Many of us expect to receive a perfectly matching picture of our dreams or we feel disappointment. This leaves no room for synchronicity to enter and fill in the blanks. What is important is always keeping your energetic lights on, and following the clues of what actually shows up in response to your vision.

Clarity in Action: Judy's Story

Judy is a professional dancer. When she began her Clarity work, she was the co-founder and leader of a well-known, small dance company of very passionate performers. It was a highly creative group; one that spent many hours rehearsing prior to their performances.

In addition to the physically tiring rehearsals, there were all sorts of pre-performance details to take care of. Every step along the way involved conflict with the other members of the troupe around creative direction. There was an incredible amount of drama around every decision, from the costumes and the sequencing of the performance to the lighting and the programs. For Judy, the whole process had become emotionally exhausting. Even though she was doing what she loved to do— dancing and performing were always lights-on for her—the last-minute drama was definitely putting her lights out.

The negative thinking of everyone involved had created an atmosphere that was draining. Judy set her intention to approach their interactions with a more positive energy and model a more effective communication style. She designed a format for the team meeting that she implemented before the next rehearsal, when everyone was fresh.

Her personal intention was to connect with the spirit, not the ego, of the people involved and to stay solution-focused and energized. She started the meeting by informing everyone of her intention and introduced the new format by having everyone focus only on what was working creatively and administratively, and what could be done differently to be more effective and less exhausting.

With Judy's leadership, the company realized how debilitating all the drama and conflict was and decided to change the way they were interacting. Following the new format, they began to set their intentions before every meeting and every performance. As a result, their next performance was very different. Everyone went into it energized and excited, instead of physically tired and emotionally drained.

Navigational Tools: Setting Your Intention

The energy and the focus of your thoughts are an important part of setting an intention. When you set your intention, it is important to think and speak in terms of what you *want* rather than what you *don't* want.

- Beware of negative thoughts and speech patterns, such as: *I should, I ought to, I have to.* These can undermine your intentions. *In every meeting I'm in today, my intention is to be fully engaged,* is a more empowering thought than: "Since I have to be in meetings all day, I should try and pay attention."

- Set clear intentions daily by using the template *My intention for today is* _____ . A positive example would be: *My intention for today is to eat healthily at all meals.* This phrasing gives you direction and fosters action. (A negative example would be *My intention for today is to not eat junk food.* This phrasing can create inertia by emphasizing what you *don't* intend to do without saying what you *do* intend to do.)

Create Attraction

As you begin to live every day intentionally, following your lights-on energy with your thoughts, actions and behaviors, you will notice that people are responding to you with similar energy. Energy attracts like energy. So, in your thoughts, words, and actions, be very clear about what you want to attract into your life.

As we said in Chapter Three, *Looking for Lights On*, when you focus your thoughts and actions in a calm, energized, lights-on state, you will look and feel different, and reflect, act, and attract differently. You will have an overall balanced, lighter, more uplifted appearance—an inner glow. You will feel more energized and move through your daily life with more grace and ease. As a result, you will act differently. Your actions will be purposeful and aligned with your vision. And you will attract more of what you want into your life.

> The old paradigm was to wait until circumstances were perfect and then act. The **new** paradigm is to act **as if** what you want is already a reality, in order to create the circumstances. If you live it like you want it to be, you will attract to you what you need to take your vision to the next level. True attraction is effortless and joy-filled.

When you send your attractor energy out into the world, you will notice that coincidences and synchronicities appear. Out of the blue, the person who can provide information for the next step in your journey will turn up at a party or networking event you attend. You are thinking about someone, and the phone rings and it's that person on the line. Watch for synchronous events to occur. They are clues that you are truly in energetic flow toward your vision. They guide you in the direction you need to go.

Clarity in Action: Justin's Story

Justin is a very successful business man. Over several years he had developed a multi-unit service business with locations in several cities. A few years after he began growing his business, he went into a partnership with Stan, intending to share the workload. Within a very short time, Justin and Stan began to disagree about almost everything. They tried for a couple of years to work out their differences, but nothing changed. Their behavior toward one another began to affect all their employees, creating a toxic work environment. Surprisingly, in spite of this toxic environment, the business continued to make money, so both partners were reluctant to make necessary changes.

By following the *Clarity* process, Justin became very clear about what he passionately wanted for himself, his family, and his employees. He returned to his work with renewed energy and an intention to create a new way of working. Every day he began to practice the *Clarity* tools and went into the office with renewed energy, a clear intention, and a belief that a winning scenario could be created for everyone, including his partner. At one point, his wife sent us a thank you note because her husband was using words like everyday miracles, intention and gratitude, and he had a renewed sense of energy and commitment to make things happen differently.

Even though Justin and Stan still disagreed about most things, Stan noticed the change in Justin's energy and commented on it. Their conversations became less combative, and several key employees told Justin how much better it felt in the office without all the negative energy.

Then synchronicity appeared. One of Justin's lights-on clues was a desire to provide consulting to other businesses that did similar work. He believed he had a lot to offer and set an intention to let people know he would be available sometime in the future. Suddenly, two different people approached him about consulting work. He had not advertised his services or told anyone about his vision. Just being lights-on about the thought of consulting opened the door for synchronicity to enter.

As time went on, Stan began his own *Clarity* journey, and he and Justin found a way to dissolve their partnership in a manner that energized them both.

Navigational Tools: Become an Attractor

Using the Energy Meter, assess the quality of your interactions, your relationships, and what you are attracting to your vision. Distinguish between attracting drama (0 on the meter), which is energy-draining, and increasing energy (10 on the meter), which is vitalizing.

- Be aware when your life seems to move forward effortlessly, as if you were being pulled along by an unseen current. Think of that current as the attraction factor.

- Notice how quickly your lights-on clues manifest into reality. Observe when people show up just as you need them, and information appears to guide your next step.

- Recognize and note intentions you have set in motion that are attracting people and information to you.

- Write down all examples of synchronous events that occur in your life.

Chapter Nine

Observing Resistance, Shifting Attention

*The real voyage of discovery consists not in seeking
new landscapes, but in having new eyes.*
—Marcel Proust, Author

 Creating attraction—the energy that draws
in the people and situations that will help
you move toward your vision—requires
that you also understand its opposite, resistance—
the magnetic field you want to steer away from.
Learning to pay attention to resistance as it appears
on your journey is critical for moving your thoughts
and actions toward attraction. As you get a feel for
the dynamic between attraction and resistance, you
will be equipped to watch for the clues that will help
you shift your attention to doing what is necessary to
get back into forward flow.

Energetic resistance can come from external forces
blocking your progress, such as a person or situation,
or it can come from within—from your own conscious

or unconscious actions. You will experience resistance as a slowing of your progress—a lack of energetic flow. Sometimes there will be so much resistance that it will stop your forward momentum completely.

It's important to pay attention to resistance when it occurs, and to use the information it contains to reassess your course of action. If you find yourself saying, "I'm going to do this no matter what," or "I'm going to do this even if it kills me," you will know that your attention and focus have gone to resistance instead of to following your lights-on energy toward your vision.

This energetic resistance will continue until you figure out what it is telling you. Is it taking your focus off committing yourself to actions that are aligned with your dream? Is it sending you a stop-and-reevaluate signal? Hard work and diligence are essential in reaching a goal, but excessive stress and pressure lead only to exhaustion, and divert you from your path.

There are many times in life when we are called to do difficult things to further our dreams and goals. It's not that every sign of difficulty or effort is a clue that you are on the wrong path. We are merely suggesting that you pay attention so you will be aware of clues as they appear. Discerning which clues spell resistance will help you make conscious choices about what action is required to best accomplish your vision.

Clarity in Action: Carl's Story

Several years ago a friend of ours, Carl, was expanding his business into other markets. He had been very successful with his small franchised retail business in the two cities where he began. At the time he believed he had proven his abilities and was driven to build what he termed a mini-conglomerate. His own internal drive dictated he acquire the rights to additional markets.

He did extensive market research on the two expansion locations both of which were located in another state. All the economics looked excellent in every category he knew to be important. After signing the franchise agreements on both markets, Carl began to look for locations to lease and employees to staff them. Then the clues of resistance began to appear.

In both cities appropriate retail space was not available. To get the space he required, he had to make several compromises. Carl was an experienced businessman, and he knew how important the right locations would be to his success. However, the fact was that to do business in these towns, he needed to compromise and settle for less than optimal space.

After several scouting trips, he ultimately decided—against his own better judgment—to sign leases and begin tenant improvements. He says now that he was so driven and confident in his ability to overcome the obstacles, he ignored his own advice and experience. He told himself he could succeed no matter what.

Then he began to interview for employees to serve his customers. More resistance showed up. After two weeks of interviewing almost 100 people, Carl had found only two who fit his definition of an ideal employee. In addition, as he was interviewing people, he received less than enthusiastic comments about the service he was bringing to the market.

As he tells it, he lay in bed one night after a long and depressing day of interviews and realized he was interviewing the local marketplace, and they didn't want his service. He determined that the smartest thing to do was to pull the plug on the whole project. He was going to do it the next day. He knew it would be difficult and expensive to cancel the leases and the franchise agreements. He says, "I went to sleep that night feeling immense relief that my little misadventure was over and it would only cost $50,000 to $75,000 to get out of it."

However, by the next morning he changed his mind. He told himself that he was just tired; that was a lot of money to give up; and he could overcome all the challenges; they were not insurmountable. He ignored the resistance clues that were blatantly obvious from the lack of available retail space and the results of his interviews.

Everything Carl realized that evening while lying in his bed was, in fact, true. He did open both locations and he then spent most of his time focusing on overcoming market resistance and dealing with less than effective employees. After an exhausting year of struggle, he sold the two locations for pennies on the dollar. It was a very expensive lesson of the effect of struggling against resistance.

Clarity in Action: Ann and John's Story

Ann and John were relocating to a new urban area and had created a vision map to guide their search for a live/work space. After months of touring properties that were close to their vision but not quite a match, they came across one that really captured their imagination. It was a carriage house behind a Victorian house to which it had once belonged. Though currently used to garage a classic car collection, it was listed as a potential residence.

Ann and John fell in love with the huge open space, the high ceilings and brick walls, and the location near downtown. The building sat on a large lot that offered unique privacy in the heart of the city. They were so excited by the potential to create a truly unique space that they hired an architect to do a preliminary design while they proceeded with the legalities of closing the deal.

The first clue of resistance came when the seller tried to insert a "Buy As Is" clause in the contract and pushed for a quick transfer of possession. Ann and John were not concerned, however, and negotiated a contract that gave them time to do the necessary inspections.

The second challenge they encountered was discovering that the water and sewer lines for the carriage house had never been separated from those of the main house. They would need to get permits from the city and hire a contractor to bring water from the city lines under the street. Still, Ann and John were not deterred; they knew there would be work involved in renovating an old building. They just knew that when it was completed they would have a wonderful little oasis in the city.

During this time, they were also selling their home in another state. When they made the offer on the carriage house, they thought their old home had sold. But just before closing, the buyer backed out, and Ann and John were forced to negotiate a later closing date on the property they were buying. This was one clue they knew they needed to pay attention to. But soon they had another buyer and were back on track.

And then they visited City Hall and found out that the carriage house was not zoned for residential use. It would require a hearing before the zoning board to secure permission. While it was likely that their request would be approved, it would be several weeks before the hearing could be scheduled. At this point, the lack of flow was so obvious to Ann and John that they stopped the sale, forfeiting the investment with the architect, and began their search anew.

But as it happened, during the months that Ann and John had spent trying to buy the carriage house, another property had come on the market that fit their vision perfectly. Even better, it was available for immediate occupancy. This time, the sale went through without a hitch, and they were able to move in quickly.

Navigational Tools: Noticing Resistance

The message from the above experiences is that in moving forward toward your vision, it's essential to be aware of the clues you are receiving, so that if necessary, you can adjust your strategy. Ask yourself:

- Are you being shown signs of flow and ease?

- Are you struggling with challenges that drain your energy?

- Is what's showing up taking your focus off actions aligned with your dream?

- Is it draining your energy?

- Is it sending you a stop-and-evaluate signal?

- Are there people or situations blocking your progress?

- Are you finding yourself doing something out of obligation or fear rather than out of enthusiasm and trust?

You might want to make a note of any clues that show up—and write down your answers to these questions—so that you won't overlook something that could slow or halt your progress.

Shift Your Attention

The way out of resistance, whether from an external source or your own internal dialogue, is to consciously shift your attention. You can move closer to making your vision a reality by shifting your focus to the thoughts and the actions that bring forward flow.

On the *Clarity* journey, the concept of "change your thinking, change your life" is all about the lights-on energy you bring to a situation. If you focus your thoughts and attention on resistance and your struggle against it, you will only bring more lights-off energy into play. You cannot make viable decisions about what actions to take from a low-energy mindset. You are far more likely to make decisions aligned with your vision and take appropriate action if you view your choices through the filter of lights-on energy.

The power of changing your thoughts to create a different reality has now been established scientifically. Studies in cellular biology and neuroscience show that the cells in your body and the neural pathways in your brain are impacted by your thoughts, both positive and negative. Each cell membrane receives a signal from the environment, and the behavior of the cell is affected by your brain's interpretation of that signal.

Where you place your attention creates new neural pathways. The power of the brain to change in response to the external and internal environment is known as neuroplasticity. Directing attention away from negative thoughts toward positive ones can create permanent changes. When you continually focus on positive thoughts and qualities like kindness, compassion, and generosity, the brain actually rewires itself so that it skews toward a more optimistic outlook, and the old, well-worn paths of negative thinking become more difficult to access.

Changing any negative habit, including negative thinking, takes sustained, conscious effort. But neuroscientists report that re-patterning the brain can take place in as little as two weeks, creating an atmosphere for growth, creativity, and lights-on behavior. When you continually shift your attention to the people and things that light you up, new neural pathways are formed that will increase your ability to stay lights-on.

Clarity in Action: Joann's Story

Following a long held vision, Joann opened a yoga studio that she operated successfully for several years. Like many creative entrepreneurs, she began to realize that managing the studio was draining her energy. She loved teaching classes and training other yoga instructors, but she did not like running the business.

Joann considered different strategies: hiring a manager, selling the studio, finding a managing partner/investor. She also considered closing the studio altogether, but she could not bring herself to abandon her loyal clients, or give up on her original dream.

She developed a new vision of using her yoga reputation to produce a local weekly television show that would present the life-enhancing practice of yoga to a wider audience. She envisioned the freedom of presenting her expertise in a way that did not keep her tied to a physical location.

Her one stumbling block was that she remained focused for months on how managing the studio was preventing her from following her bigger dream, and she couldn't let go of the idea that she had to keep the studio open even if she no longer wanted to run it. Joann's old thought patterns continued to drain her energy and blocked her ability to see other possibilities.

When she finally realized that her resistance was preventing her from realizing her dream, Joann committed to shifting her focus to her more expansive vision. Every time she began to think about what she couldn't do, she immediately refocused her thoughts on her intention to create something new.

Although she was still involved with daily management tasks, Joann felt more energized because she began to see possibilities. Holding the vision of what she wanted to create, she was able to see her current situation in a more forgiving light. New ideas began to percolate, and it occurred to her that she could create a new way of serving her long term clients. Rather than sell the studio and the brand name she had spent so long developing, she saw that she could trade on her brand to launch her expanded venture.

Joann didn't need her own studio to continue serving her clients; she could rent other studios in which to hold classes. She also saw that closing the studio didn't mean failure. She was simply expanding and evolving her business. Shifting her attention to this expanded vision every time she got stuck in feelings of limitation enabled her to see new ways of achieving her dream.

Navigational Tools: Shifting Your Attention

As Joann's experience illustrates, consciously shifting your attention to lights-on thoughts and behaviors creates energetic flow. This is a good time to use rapid discovery and rapid recovery.

- Ask yourself, *Where are my thoughts right now?* If they are coming from fear, doubt, or some other negative energy, immediately turn your attention to something positive. To find something positive to focus on, think of someone or something for which you are grateful. Feeling and expressing gratitude brings lights-on energy into your system. Looking at your vision map and experiencing the energy of what you have envisioned help you shift your thoughts.

- Keep notes or write in your journal about what happens to your energy when you shift your attention to something positive. Over time, you will begin to notice that you are less likely to get caught up in old, lights-off thoughts and you are able to shift to more effective thoughts much more rapidly.

Chapter Ten

Navigating Choice Points

Once you replace negative thoughts with positive ones,
you'll start having positive results.
—Willie Nelson, Singer Philosopher

Every outcome in present time is the result of a decision made at a choice point, or pivotal moment, in the past. Our choices create our current reality. From moment to moment, situations arise that require us to make choices. The way in which we focus our attention in those instances is what we call "navigating choice points." Though navigating choice points, or transitions, at times may seem perplexing or stressful, these are actually key opportunities to consider different possibilities and make decisions that move you closer to your vision.

In daily life, as on the *Clarity* journey, divergent channels are constantly appearing, requiring choices on everything from what to eat and what to wear to where to live and how to communicate an idea. All these choice points require focused attention. In every instance, the goal is to choose above-the-line thoughts and actions—those that are energizing and solution-oriented—rather than under-the-line thoughts and actions that are draining and problem-focused.

On this journey, you are clearly seeking transformation and change. So what does that mean in the action phase of the journey, when it's time to launch your vision? The word "transform" will give you a clue. *Trans* is Latin for "change"; to transform is to change your form, or state. And in order to transform, you have to come undone and then reform in a new way.

Most of our formal education and training fails to address the issue of change, and few of us learn enough about deep change to be comfortable with it. And today, transition, transformation, and change are occurring more rapidly than at any other time in history. This acceleration makes it imperative to learn new skills for rapidly redesigning your guiding vision and the strategy to achieve it as you are faced with choice points.

Just in the past decade, the deluge of information offered by new technology requires us to become more fluid and adaptive in our decision-making than our predecessors. A century ago, when there were fewer choice points, with more time in between them, humans adapted to change in concert with natural cycles—the rhythm of waking and sleeping, the flow of seasons, birth and death. Today, however, we no longer have the leisure to wait for change to occur naturally.

In order to navigate the rest of the *Clarity* journey with ease and grace—to find it exciting, not frightening—there is something you need to know: transition is a natural part of the change process. It creates a *liminal zone,* an "in between" or threshold, in which you're no longer where you were but not yet where you're going. Visions by their very nature are constantly evolving. They morph or shape-shift as information is added or subtracted.

A key skill for successful journeying is learning to navigate this transition zone—to be comfortable with uncertainty and living the mystery, as you follow your vision. This requires trusting that once you have a clear strategy for navigating choice points, a new, more evolved vision will emerge to guide you on the next leg of your journey.

On the *Clarity Attention Guide* at the end of this chapter, the transition line is the bridge between above-the-line and under-the-line behaviors and thoughts. Every time you shift your attention from under-the-line to above-the-line, you cross through this zone and can experience some or all of the behaviors common to transition: discomfort, frustration, shift, transformation, challenge, and paradox. When you find yourself sensing any of these experiences, it is a clue that you are at a choice point, and you can choose to take your attention above or below the line.

> (◎) **A key skill for successful journeying is learning to navigate the transition zone—being relaxed with being in between and comfortable with living the mystery as you follow your vision.**

The transition zone is the zone of transformation, where the choices you make determine the results of your actions. Above-the-line choices are those that are energizing, passionate, and solution focused, while under-the-line choices simply continue old patterns that are draining and problem-focused resulting in limited possibilities and stagnation. To stay true to your vision, it is essential to focus your choices above the line and choose passion and lights-on.

Clarity in Action: Stan's Story

We mentioned Stan earlier in Justin's story. Prior to becoming Justin's partner, Stan had his own successful business for several years. Although he was successful, he hated the management and marketing involved in building and maintaining the revenue and client base. What he did love and was very good at doing was delivering the technical services to his customers. When he and Justin were discussing becoming partners, Stan was excited by the possibility of turning the management and marketing over to Justin and devoting all his time to being the technician and taking care of the customers.

Shortly after they began operating under the new partnership agreement, they disagreed about almost everything to do with how to manage the business, how to market their services, how to train and develop employees, basically how to do everything except customer service. Stan and Justin would spend hours creating an understanding about some new aspect of the business. Justin would leave the meeting believing they were in agreement. Stan would leave the meeting and not follow through on what was agreed upon. And then they were back into arguing or not communicating at all. This went on for several years.

As Stan began to understand and apply the *Clarity* principles, he realized that while he didn't want to do the management of the business, he also had a huge need to control what was done. If he didn't have control, he was fearful of the effect someone else's management would have on his income. Even though Stan was making more money than he had in his previous business, he couldn't let go of the fear and trust issues of having Justin be responsible for managing. This need to control all aspects kept him fearful of anything Justin suggested or attempted to put into place. He would then become distrustful and doubting about all of it. Obviously, this would lead to more lack of trust, an inability to communicate and as mentioned previously, it created a toxic work environment for everyone.

When Stan recognized how his behavior and thoughts were contributing to the situation, he began to use *rapid discovery, rapid recovery* whenever he found himself feeling out of control or fearful of the way the business was being managed. This didn't mean he didn't question or challenge anything he had questions about.

What did begin to happen, however, was that after he received the information he requested, he focused his thoughts and energy on empowering Justin's decisions and trusting the process. This dramatically changed everything. By merely changing his energetic response to all of the management issues, the energy and flow of the business began to change.

Clarity in Action: Elaina's Story

As she began her *Clarity* journey, Elaina became aware that her day-to-day decision-making was based on some long-standing shadow or under-the-line behaviors. With new awareness, she began to practice *rapid discovery* and *rapid recovery* every time she found herself reacting to events out of those old patterns.

Elaina had been divorced for several years and shared custody of her two children with her ex-husband. Many aspects of that arrangement had upset her for years, causing a lot of drama that always left her frustrated and exhausted. She was determined to change her behavior. Before every interaction with her children's father, she started setting an intention to stay lights-on—to observe when her thoughts and behavior created drama and drained her energy, and to shift those thoughts immediately.

She also began to practice *sacred selfishness*, asking herself what she really wanted the custody arrangement to be. Elaine realized that she had sacrificed her own needs and desires when the initial custody agreement was drawn up. It turned out that not only had that agreement never worked for her, but it hadn't served the needs of her children either.

Focusing her attention on what she wanted helped Elaina renegotiate the existing custody arrangement to fit her needs and her children's. She approached the situation from the viewpoint that all things are possible and there was a solution that would serve them all. As often happens, when she focused her thoughts on keeping her energy and behavior above-the-line, the result was positive for everyone involved.

Navigational Tools:
Navigating Choice Points

In every moment you are presented with choice points (either above or below the line). They are a universal constant. You are in charge of your choices. The challenge is to remain mindful and aware of what your options are and to always choose *passion over pattern*.

The *Clarity Attention Guide* below will help you determine whether or not you are choosing lights-on and passion when making decisions, or lights-off and limiting patterns. If the words above the line match your actions, then you have chosen well. You can reference the bridge in the lower left corner of the *Get Clarity Journey Map* to see clearly how choosing above-the-line will keep you in flow. Beware of choosing familiar patterns out of habit. Study the Attention Guide to find out where you are, and if it looks like you are stuck under-the-line, then shift your attention to an above-the-line thought or action, and get back into flow.

How to Use the Clarity Attention Guide

This guide and balance sheet is another *Clarity* tool to help you stay conscious and mindful about the choices you make and the behaviors you exhibit. When you are consciously aware, you will not

CLARITY ATTENTION GUIDE AND BALANCE SHEET

	INDIVIDUALS *What is my energy at work characterized by?*	LEADERS *Where is my energy focused as a leader?*	
◆	Effortlessness	Service	◆
✳	High Noticing	Visionary	✳
●	Authenticity	Acknowledging	●
★	Dedication	Coaching	★
◉	Enthusiasm	Modeling	◉
⌘	Excitement	Confidence	⌘
■	Trust	Honesty	■
	Discomfort	Frustration	
■	Fear	Manipulating	■
⌘	Exhaustion	Sabotaging	⌘
◉	Anxiety	Evaluating	◉
★	Defiance	Telling	★
●	Self-Importance	Advising	●
✳	Habituation	Assuming	✳
◆	Overdoing	Dictatorial	◆

EFFECTIVE
Solution Focused

CHOICE POINT

INEFFECTIVE
Problem Focused

EFFECTIVE
Flow

THE TRANSITION
LINE

INEFFECTIVE
Eddy

intentionally make ineffective choices about your behaviors. This guide is put in chart form to make shifting your attention quick and easy.

Looking at the column for individuals, there is a column of fourteen words with corresponding symbols to the left, and there is a line dividing the fourteen words. The dividing line containing the word discomfort is the transition line.

The upper half of the guide contains a collection of seven words representing above-the-line thoughts and behaviors. Energetically, above-the-line represents the field of possibilities. It is lights-on and effective. We also refer to above-the-line as the *light side*. Actions initiated from this field are referred to as solution focused and effective as opposed to good or right.

The lower half of the guide contains a collection of seven words representing under-the-line thoughts and behaviors. Energetically, below the line represents the *field of limits*. It is lights-off and ineffective. *We also refer to under-the-line as the shadow side or shadow behavior.* Actions initiated from this field are referred to as problem focused and ineffective as opposed to bad or wrong.

The transition line is the bridge between the groups. Every time you shift your attention from under-the-line to above-the-line, you cross through this zone and can experience some or all of the behaviors common to transition: discomfort, frustration, shift, transformation, challenge, and paradox. When you find yourself sensing any of these experiences, it is a clue that you are at a choice point and you can choose to take your attention above or below the line.

The symbols (i.e. ✻) are used to show a connection between a specific under-the-line behavior and a specific above-the-line behavior.

Example of how the vertical fields operate:

Fear (■ below) is the shadow side of **trust** (■ above) and discomfort (on the bridge) is the transitional experience.

Anxiety (◉ below) is the shadow side of **enthusiasm** (◉ above) and discomfort (on the bridge) is the transitional experience.

Defiance (★ below) is the shadow side of **dedication** (★ above) and discomfort (on the bridge) is the transitional experience.

Chapter Eleven

Launching Your Vision

Vision without action is a daydream.
Action without vision is a nightmare.
—Japanese Proverb

Until now, you have been focusing on your vision—the *what*—and not on the *how-to*—of your method for achieving it. The initial energy-detecting is behind you, and you are ready to go forward. It is time to put your boat in the water—put your vision into action—and get into the deep water of your journey. What does it take to initiate a vision? A strategy, complete with action steps. Action steps create the momentum to realize your vision; therefore, all of your action steps must be energizing and create excitement as you anticipate their result. That excitement makes the movement in the direction of your dream seem effortless—and timeless.

Almost without exception, our clients report that as they launched their new vision, it seemed as if time stood still. This phase of the journey is a very energizing time, filled with a mixture of fear and excitement: you're taking a leap of faith. At this point, self-actualized people—those who are living the fulfillment of their dreams—say that courage is the key component. They faced their fears and moved forward regardless. And they moved forward with a vision and strategy, just as you are about to do.

Your tools for putting your vision into action are the vision map you made earlier—updated with your discoveries from previous exercises—and the action steps you are about to identify.

Once you have tuned up your vision and designed your strategy, you will be ready to launch. We use a model called a *Bridge Plan* to provide a structure for this stage. The *Bridge Plan* is dynamic and ever-changing as you add and delete information over the course of your journey. This dynamic model will help you maintain forward momentum as you swing between vision and action: here is where I am now; here is where I want to be. What are the lights-on actions to get me there?

Creating in Action: Ellen's Story

When Ellen entered the *Get Clarity* retreat, she was exhausted and dragging through the day. She felt thoroughly depleted at the end of her usual seventy-hour work week. Her career as director of a large non-profit organization was very demanding, and she had almost no energy left for her husband and two daughters.

While working downtown, she imagined a place where she could get a relaxing spa treatment during her lunch hour. But there was no spa near her office that offered high-quality services in under an hour. During her visioning session, Ellen became very clear that she wanted to start a downtown day spa within walking distance of most offices, where clients could receive unique, 25-minute "express" services.

Ellen's first action step was to share her vision with her husband whose support was necessary to initiate any change of that magnitude. A new business would be a risk to their financial security, and there was much to consider, since neither Ellen nor David had any experience as an entrepreneur. They had always been employees with job security and benefits.

Both were in their late forties and anticipated early retirement in ten years. But at the rate she was working, Ellen wasn't sure if she could physically and emotionally survive the stress of her job until retirement. It was imperative that she find a way to make her dream come true without risking their life savings.

Ellen needed to do some in-depth research into what would be entailed in creating a spa. She spent the next year on this preparatory homework, gathering information about costs to start a day spa, the time it would take to become profitable, and the demographics for an ideal location. Ellen enjoyed the research process and found it very energizing— not at all like her regular job.

The next step was a coaching session in which Ellen and David created a bridge plan, balancing two key facts that had emerged from her research. Creating a spa was going to be very costly, but at the same time, Ellen's day-spa concept was at the forefront of an emerging business trend, making it, in all likelihood, a savvy investment. Guided by both the numbers and her passion to do it, Ellen went ahead with initiating her vision.

Given her lack of entrepreneurial expertise, it was a total leap of faith. She and David had fears and challenges to overcome, but they were confident their enterprise would be successful. However, had Ellen tried to implement her strategy before she was crystal clear about her vision, her fear of the large investment and her lack of experience might have depleted her energy. Without the pulling power of her vision, those fears could have stopped before she even started. As it was, Ellen's preparation paid off, and their day spa opened to great success— clearly filling a need in the downtown business community.

Navigational Tools: Creating an Action Plan

Your next step toward launching your vision is to create an action plan:

- Hang your vision map where you can see it easily, as a constant reminder of where you are headed.

- Make a list of what you want to create in your life, combining all your lights-on clues from the previous chapters. Then, next to the list, write down the action steps needed to achieve each aspect of your vision.

- Create an action plan by prioritizing the action steps.

- Using the diagram below as a template, create a Bridge Plan. On the bridge, place the action steps that are energizing and will move you closer to your goal. If you have any action steps that are necessary but don't light you up, create a plan for delegating those actions to someone else.

**Here's where
you are now.**

**Here's where you
want to go—
your lights-on vision**

Fill in some action items on the bridge that are energizing and will move you closer to your vision.

Remember that all action steps in present time should be in service to your vision. This avoids busy work.

PART IV

Correct Course

Chapter Twelve

Cruising through Challenges

By banishing doubt and trusting your intuitive feelings,
you clear a space for the power of intention to flow through.
—Wayne Dyer, Author and Speaker

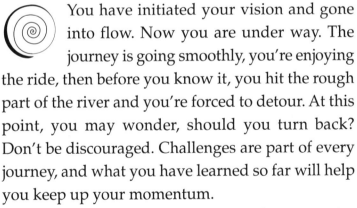 You have initiated your vision and gone into flow. Now you are under way. The journey is going smoothly, you're enjoying the ride, then before you know it, you hit the rough part of the river and you're forced to detour. At this point, you may wonder, should you turn back? Don't be discouraged. Challenges are part of every journey, and what you have learned so far will help you keep up your momentum.

A detour can be any divergence from your intended route. On the *Get Clarity Journey Map* (located in the back of the book), it is symbolized by a log jam. Often you will hit a metaphorical log jam when you start sharing your dream with others. People are only too willing to offer advice and opinions on what you should be doing: "That's a good idea *but* ..." or "If *I* were you ..." As you listen to this unsolicited advice, you may notice yourself starting to feel drained or irritable.

No matter how well intended, others' opinions can knock your lights out and knock you off course. Feedback, however, is a different story. It is a natural part of any energetic operating system. Feedback mirrors your enthusiasm back to you. It's an astute observer saying, "I can see that your vision lights you up; tell me more about it."

The way to get out of a log jam and back into flow is to find someone to give you effective feedback. Look for a person who is willing to suspend judgment and forgo opinions and advice, and simply report what they notice energizes you, then reflect it back to you. A support person who gives reflective feedback rather than projecting their unsolicited opinions and advice onto you, is an important strategic ally. It's very helpful to have at least one unbiased person like this on your team. Accurate feedback is not about someone else's ideas for you— only about what lights you up.

When you're faced with so-called "friendly" advice, remember not to take it personally. Well-meaning people may think they're "protecting" you, but they're really only projecting their own fears. Don't let their issues prevent you from initiating your vision.

Clarity in Action: Susan's Story

While Susan was working as a school counselor and getting a Master's degree in counseling, she created a game to be used in the classroom. The purpose of the game was to foster connection and promote deeper conversation among the participants, with the goal of reducing alienation and violence. Susan envisioned using the game to assist students in developing relationship skills.

She made the first game board out of felt that she cut and sewed herself. When she introduced the game into the classroom, it was very well received, and many teachers and counselors requested copies. It soon became clear that the demand was enough for Susan to create a business producing the game. But if she was going to be an entrepreneur and go into production while still working full-time as a counselor, she knew she would need a business plan and money to get started.

Susan entered the *Get Clarity* retreat to sharpen her business vision and determine how she wanted to do the production, as well as figure out what instructional materials she would need to include for people who intended to facilitate the game for others. She was adamant that she wanted the game to have a hand-crafted look, and she envisioned supporting her community by using local craftspeople.

Susan left the retreat with a very clear vision of how she wanted to do all aspects of her business. But when she presented her ideas to some business consultants, she hit her first detour. Based on their analysis, they said that in order for the business to be profitable, Susan would need to manufacture the game overseas. She was determined, however, to stick to her vision of using local craftspeople, and spent months working with the financial numbers to make her business plan appeal to the bank. She kept getting her lights knocked out as she repeatedly ran into negativity from bankers and business advisors alike.

Susan began to question her original dream; maybe she could go into production overseas after all. But every time she expressed that thought to her coach or support team, she received the same feedback: "That knocks your lights out." She was so obviously lights-on about local production that they encouraged her to continue looking for ways to finance her original vision.

In the months of trying unsuccessfully to negotiate a bank loan that didn't require overseas production, Susan fine-tuned her business plan until she was confident that she could be profitable. With the support of a professor from her graduate program, she decided to approach private investors. After the months of energy-draining number-crunching, she finally shifted her attention back to her vision and created the attraction energy she needed. Ultimately, an angel investor who shared her vision of producing the game locally showed up with financial support.

Susan's business is now fully operational and providing a valuable service nationally and internationally. And true to her vision, she is producing it with local people, each of whom she personally knows. Susan successfully steered her dream through a series of challenges and remained true to her vision of honoring community and personal connections with a production process that mirrors total integrity.

Navigational Tools: Handling Detours

Detours are part of every *Clarity* journey. So what do you do when you hit one?

- Return to your vision. Refocus your energy by studying your vision map. Make sure you are looking at all the information through the filter of your vision so that you are always giving it an energetic perspective. Keep your thoughts and actions above the line, as you create a strategy to get around the detour.

- If you need extra help with the process, find someone to act as a mirror to your vision.

Ask that person to give you accurate
feedback, observing your lights-on energy
as you state your vision. Take note of the
feedback you're given and integrate into
your new plan.

Doubt, Worry, and Negative Self-Talk

Sometimes it's not input from others that knocks your
lights out but your own monkey mind speaking to
you with doubt or worry. Going through a major
transition is seldom comfortable and may raise
doubt and fear of the unknown.

> **There can be moments on the Clarity
> journey when you are uncertain about
> what choice to make or what action to take.
> At such times it's essential not to lose sight
> of the fact that self-criticism, worry, and
> doubt will never give you accurate
> information on which to base decisions.
> They will only increase your fear and lead
> to inertia as you vacillate.**

Doubt and worry take you out of the present
moment and into overdramatizing past experiences—
we call this *fictional history tripping*—or inventing
scary stories about the future. We call that *fictional
future tripping*. Monkey mind, that self-critical inner

voice that conjures up worst-case scenarios, can stop you from pursuing your vision with running commentary like, "What was I thinking?", "I can't possibly do this" or "This will never work."

The way to deal with monkey mind is to doubt your doubt, not your dream. Fear takes over when you don't have enough information to make an intelligent choice. *Reduce your fear of the unknown by shifting your attention to gathering information.*

Clarity in Action: Matt's Story

Matt's experience is an example of how doubt and negative self-talk can nearly derail a dream. Matt is a very talented musician. After graduating from college, he played guitar with local artists, both on stage and in the studio. He was highly regarded in the local music community and developed a reputation as the go-to guitarist for high-quality studio recording.

When a well-known entertainment company announced a local audition for a new show opening in Los Angeles, Matt and several hundred other guitarists showed up. As luck and talent would have it, he was one of the very few called back for further screening the next day.

Matt was very excited about the possibility of being part of the show with all its benefits, both creative and financial. But he was also hesitant because it would mean a big change for him and his fiancée, Ann. The move to Los Angeles would require

Ann to close her successful consulting business and re-establish herself with a new clientele. There was a lot to consider if he were chosen.

Matt's monkey mind, sensing a big change coming, went into overdrive. It kept him awake all night with thoughts like, "You're no good", "You'll never make it" and "You don't deserve a big break like this." By the next morning, Matt had decided not to bother going to the audition because he wasn't good enough to be chosen. The job wasn't even a good fit for him, he rationalized. Overnight, monkey mind had convinced him not only that he didn't deserve to get the job but that he didn't want it anyway.

Luckily, Matt mentioned his decision to Ann, who called us immediately for some emergency coaching. With coaching and feedback about his lights-on clues, Matt saw that he had nothing to lose in auditioning and everything to gain. He made it to the audition literally at the last minute—and was hired on the spot for the new show.

Matt and Ann still faced the challenge of relocating her business, but she was excited about the future and began the process of finding new clients through her network of colleagues. She also researched the neighborhoods that were desirable from a live/work perspective and had fun finding them a new home.

The move has been positive for them both. Within six months of setting up at the new location,

Ann's business was back to the level she wanted. And Matt loves the show and the financial stability it provides while leaving him time to work on other creative projects. Now living his dream, Matt is still amazed to think he almost let negative self-talk take him out of the game.

Clarity in Action: Richard's Story

Richard has operated a successful optometric practice for several years. He was successful in spite of being in a restrictively small retail space. For years he had imagined how wonderful it would be for him, his staff and his patients if he had three or four times more space.

Knowing his lease was up in another year, Richard began to dream about new space and creating a new experience for his patients. He had a very clear image of what he wanted including more exam lanes, space for new technology, a larger area for displaying new frames and a totally new appearance to attract more patients.

He was very enthusiastic about the new possibilities for growing his practice and achieving the vision he had when he opened the doors several years earlier. He sat down one evening and sketched out what he termed "A wonderful office with beautiful cabinetry, wide aisles, large exam rooms, great natural light, and new equipment and technology: my dream space." With this enthusiasm Richard began to talk with other optometrists in a professional peer group he belonged to. Many of them had been through successfully expanding their practice and had always encouraged Richard to do the same. Every one of them had increased their revenue and improved their practice.

Richard gathered all the facts, looked at the financials, talked to contractors and met with his banker. It was a large investment and a long term commitment but everything pointed to it delivering a profitable boost to his revenue and bringing a new level of excitement to his business. More importantly, it would finally be the kind of facility he had dreamed of for years. And yet, he dithered.

Doubt happened. He couldn't take the next step. Thinking of all that could go wrong, he hit the wall of inertia. With a little coaching and feedback on what truly energized him, Richard began to shift his attention by gathering information that supported his vision. The first step was to doubt his doubt not his dream. Then he asked some questions:

> Would the expansion allow him to better
> serve his patients with new technology?
> Would it create more efficient patient flow?
> Was his market area growing with new
> residents moving in?
> Was there risk in staying in his small space?
> Would the move rejuvenate him and his staff?

Would he have the space to hire another
optometrist?

Would he enjoy coming into the new space
every morning?

Richard quit dithering and expanded successfully.

Navigational Tools:
Silencing Doubt and Self-Talk

Don't let negative self-talk take you out of the game.
Take specific action:

- Quiet monkey mind by listening to what
the doubt and fear are really saying. Write
down the predominant thoughts. Read
over your statements and decide if any of
those concerns are real—and need to be
addressed—or are only imagined.

- Face fear of the unknown by gathering
as much information as you can. Armed
with information, you can pursue your
vision with more certainty and less fear. If
you are considering relocating, for example,
you might explore the possibilities by
searching the Internet, consulting a realtor,
studying a map, talking to people who live
in the area, contacting the local Chamber of
Commerce, investigating community

services, and looking into employment opportunities.

Shadow Patterns

Shadow patterns are energy patterns, largely unconscious, that stop you from being in flow. *Shadow behaviors* are a metaphor for information that is hidden and cognitively difficult to see, and if you are not aware of them, they can prevent you from realizing your full potential. *Light patterns* are defined as what energizes you, and gets you into flow. *Shadow patterns* are defined as what will stop you, by creating inertia. Using an old movie metaphor, it is like recognizing your Luke Skywalker tendencies and your Darth Vader tendencies (the light and dark side characters from *Star Wars*).

Lack of knowledge of your shadow pattern (dark side) is a major factor in stopping you from realizing your full potential. The more clarity you have about your light and shadow patterns, the easier it will be to recognize your shadow patterns.

Light patterns are those that energize you and get you into flow. Examples are:

trust	enthusiasm
self-esteem	cooperation
generosity	innovation
innocence	perfection
curiosity	manifestation

faith   playfulness
vision   service

Shadow patterns are energy patterns that stop you. Examples are:

fear   envy
doubt   competition
obligation   compromise
self-pity   attachment
anxiety   martyrdom
guilt   imitation

All people who successfully manifest their visions recognize—rapid discovery—and move past their shadow behavior by having a willingness to switch focus back to lights-on energy—rapid recovery. They then go into action by doing any action that lights them up.

> **This is a simple truth—if you follow your light, you will get more light, more energy. When you do something that is energizing, you will get more energy. It's that basic.**

Remember that the shadow is always there—it never goes away. The empowerment strategy is to be truthful about when you are in your shadow, and quickly shift your attention to your journey.

Clarity in Action: Terry's Story

Terry, a certified event planner, has a big vision to create an educational and networking venue for women to connect and support their personal and professional growth. Her business includes an annual retreat as well as several other meeting opportunities throughout the year. It is a very complex business that includes arranging the events, contracting with educational speakers and meeting venues, and enrolling sponsors as well as selling memberships. For the first few years, Terry did it all herself with the help of a small group of dedicated volunteers. As the organization grew, Terry became more and more overwhelmed with all that had to be done.

As she began to apply *Clarity* concepts to her leadership style and her organization, she became aware of the impact her unconscious shadow behavior was having on her health and effectiveness. She realized that her particular shadow behavior was overdoing. She had too much on her plate and for years had been doing much of the event work herself, plus taking care of the needs of her family. When she was operating from her shadow of overdoing, she couldn't see any other possibilities for getting everything done. From that perspective, she believed she needed to be doing it all herself. Physically, it was taking a toll. As she began to reflect on how she worked, she realized that she often had migraine headaches just as the results of her hard work were being realized.

Terry began to shift her focus to more effective thoughts and behaviors. As a result, she was able to see many different possibilities for more work to be done by others while she still provided her unique leadership perspective to what was being created. This new realization allowed her to focus on trusting others while continually reflecting on how everything could be done from a feeling of effortlessness. This shift in her focus has opened her mind to seeing unlimited possibilities and creative strategies. Her business continues to grow and her migraines have almost totally disappeared.

Navigational Tools: Shifting Shadow Patterns

Shifting your thoughts and behaviors from shadow patterns begins with simply noticing where your thoughts and behaviors are. Do you behave above-the-line or below it?

- First, be easy with recognizing your shadow behavior; simply notice where you are—rapid discovery. Where are your

thoughts? How are you behaving? Study
the *Clarity Attention Guide* found on page 113
for clues.

- Then shift your thoughts above-the-line—
  rapid recovery. If you are anxious, shift your
  focus to enthusiasm. Put your attention to
  thinking about what enthusiasm at this
  moment would feel like? Pay attention to
  the energy change you feel. Commit to and
  act from that place. What do you have to do
  to create enthusiasm? Observe the different
  result you create and experience.

- You can throw a dart above-the-line and
  pick any word to focus your attention on.
  It doesn't have to be the exact opposite of
  your under-the-line thought. What's
  important is that you shift your thoughts,
  your behavior and your energy to more
  effective above-the-line patterns.

Chapter Thirteen
Embracing Eddies

That's the reason they're called lessons,
because they lesson from day to day.
—Lewis Carroll, Author

Doubt, fear, and well-intended but misguided advice are not the only challenges you are likely to face in navigating your *Clarity* journey. As you adjust your course, you are bound to encounter eddies—energetic setbacks that are pictured as whirlpools on the *Get Clarity Journey Map*. An eddy prevents you from moving forward toward your vision by spinning you around and around in place, in a familiar pattern.

Patterns are simply manifestations of lessons you need to learn. An eddy contains information and, therefore, provides a tutorial in a lesson you need to learn. Lessons tend to be repeated again and again, until you change your response. There's no stigma attached to being caught in an eddy. On the contrary, it's a golden opportunity to experience the pattern in a different way and move closer to mastering the underlying lesson.

When you find yourself swirling around in an eddy, the above-the-line question to ask yourself is, "What is the lesson here?" or "What information am I getting that will help me make a different choice?" An under-the-line question would be something like, "What's wrong here?" If you focus on what's wrong, you invite self-judgment, criticism, and blame—of others as well as yourself. A negative focus will seldom give you an answer that moves you forward toward your vision.

Instead of searching for reasons, become an observer. Stay curious about your experience. Assume nothing. The less certain you are about what's happening, the more open you will be to seeing all the possibilities. Quantum physics tells us that the observer affects what is observed; your thoughts about a situation influence the outcome. So, as much as possible, suspend thinking. Over-reliance on your left-brain analytic skills dulls intuition, a right-brain function. Balancing both sides of the brain will give you access to whole-brain intelligence, sharpening your observation skills.

When you're caught in an eddy, attention and energy are what will keep you afloat so that you can recognize patterns that are no longer of service to you; then release them and return to your path.

Practicing gratitude for the opportunity to work through a pattern will also help navigate an eddy with greater ease.

When you finally kick out of an eddy, you will be stronger and wiser for the experience. You will have tapped into deep inner reserves and learned to hold your vision no matter what. The process is not unlike what happens on a real river journey, where the reward for kicking out of an eddy may be uncovering the rich mineral deposits that lie just downstream.

We do a communication exercise in our workshops called pilot/co-pilot. Its purpose is to focus on creating effective communication between people and within and among teams. For the players this exercise almost always points out a less effective communication pattern that plays out in their work or personal life.

In a recent workshop as we were debriefing what had occurred, one of the players said, when she asked for clarification, her partner kept repeating the same words only louder. Her partner said that her business associates have told her that she does this frequently at work, especially under stress. It is an unconscious, patterned response to a request for more clarity about what she was saying.

She immediately wondered why she does that and where she learned it. Asking why may be informative at some level; however, it does not necessarily provide useful strategies for changing the behavior. And, it invites judgment and criticism that provide little guidance. The question to ask is: *What is the lesson here?* In her case, it was to focus on becoming more conscious, more present, more self aware when communicating during times of stress. She determined to create a strategy that would remind her of this and raise a red flag to remind her to get present whenever she began to repeat herself in a louder voice.

Clarity in Action: George's Story

George is a team leader in a global consulting company. He takes great pride in being very responsive to his client's needs. When a client calls, George's first reaction is to drop everything and handle this new client emergency. Unfortunately, this reactive pattern exhausts him and burns out his team. George said that his career success was built on being responsive and doing whatever was needed to serve the client. However, he was also aware of the pressure this manner of working put on him and his team. It had happened with other teams over the years.

George was in the eddy of over-reacting. He determined the lesson he needed to learn was that being of service involved more than quick responsiveness. He also needed to discover a more effective way of responding to client requests; to have an established team strategy of how to handle the emergency client needs; to delegate more effectively; and to create a communication strategy with his team that would provide him early notice when he slipped into his old pattern. As a result of being more conscious and paying attention to the pattern, George has created a team approach to more efficiently handle the work, and built systems to create more flow when getting things done. He and his team actually work less hours and get more done with reduced pressure.

As you know, changing long held behaviors is not always easy. When the behavior you want to change raises its ugly head once again, you may have tendency to voice self-judgment and be critical of why you did it again. This is never a successful approach to changing that pattern behavior.

 Self criticism is seldom an effective agent of behavior change.

It's important that you always express gratitude when you are revisiting a pattern. Practicing gratitude enhances ease and grace. If you are in an eddy revisiting a pattern, you will know that you haven't yet learned what you need to learn from that situation or person. In this awareness, be grateful because when the lesson is learned, you may not have to repeat the lesson again.

Clarity in Action: Linda's Story

Linda was a partner in a five-person consulting firm in a metropolitan area. The firm was financially successful largely because she personally conducted the initial client interviews. She had a natural style, a love of meeting people and was a magnet for new business. Attraction marketing was her expertise. Her partners depended on her to bring in new business as well as to consult with clients once they were enrolled.

After several years, however, Linda lost interest in her consultant role. During the *Clarity* process she was coached to pay attention and note whenever she felt energized in her work. By staying curious and observing her energy, she noticed that she was very lights-on whenever she was speaking in public and promoting entrepreneurs who had powerful visions. It became clear that what she wanted to do was locate individuals with big visions and coach them in launching their own businesses. With her partners' support, she took a sabbatical from her firm to pursue her interest and opened her own coaching practice.

She expected a decline in income once she went out on her own, but the decline was sharper than anticipated. Since she was responsible for bringing in half of her family's income, the decline caused stress at home. After six months, she realized that being on her own was not going to work.

Linda returned to her position at the firm and immediately fell into a familiar behavior pattern—just like falling into an eddy on the *Get Clarity Journey Map*. Stepping back in was an easy transition, but as she was lulled back into the familiar pattern, it became increasingly harder for her to stay sharp and creative. Linda sensed, however, that she was back in the old pattern in order to learn a lesson about being true to herself.

After three months of swirling in that eddy, becoming progressively bored and drained, Linda decided to drop any preconceived ideas about the job and just observe her energy. She shifted her attention to what lit her up, telling herself, "I'm okay, there's nothing seriously knocking me out here, but I'm falling asleep and that's not okay. What I really want to do aside from public speaking is write a book about brilliant enterprises. I want to honor this calling and be true to myself."

Linda again resigned from the partnership and started writing. She kicked out of the eddy and uncovered the gold downstream—and felt stronger and wiser for the experience. Soon thereafter, she found a business partner who wanted to invest in publishing. In addition to publishing books about entrepreneurship, they promote exciting entrepreneurial projects, or as Linda envisioned, "brilliant enterprises."

Presently, Linda is doing the public speaking for the firm, and she has published her book on entrepreneurs. She has financial flow, which has improved her family relations, and she is very lights-on about her work.

Navigational Tools: Embracing an Eddy

One popular definition of insanity is repeating the same behavior over and over and expecting different results. A classic example is repeatedly getting involved in relationships with the same type of person who always breaks your heart. An eddy provides an opportunity to kick an old pattern once and for all.

- Make a list of the patterns you recognize are operating in your life and the lesson or lessons that each represents.

- Pick the pattern you feel is most detrimental to your energy and to achieving your vision. Create an action step or strategy to break the pattern. Write it down in the form of an intention and make a commitment to taking action to change your approach.

- Be an observer. Stay curious, and adopt *beginner's mind*: look at all people and situations as if they are brand new to you.

- Practice gratitude. It will help you navigate eddies with ease and grace. Reflect on the lessons you have learned so far on the *Clarity* journey. Express gratitude for what you have learned. Be grateful for what you have learned and for the fact that you may not have to repeat the pattern. Write a gratitude statement about each person who has helped you learn those lessons.

PART V

Sail Home

Chapter Fourteen

Staying in the Present

You must live in the present, launch yourself on every wave, find your eternity in each moment. Fools stand on their island opportunities and look toward another land. There is no other land, there is no other life but this.
—Henry David Thoreau, Author and Naturalist

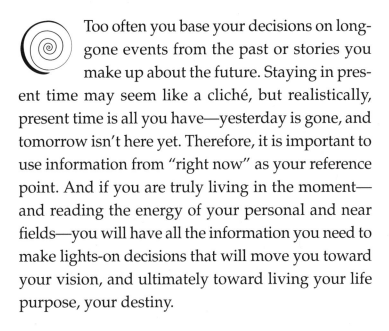 Too often you base your decisions on long-gone events from the past or stories you make up about the future. Staying in present time may seem like a cliché, but realistically, present time is all you have—yesterday is gone, and tomorrow isn't here yet. Therefore, it is important to use information from "right now" as your reference point. And if you are truly living in the moment— and reading the energy of your personal and near fields—you will have all the information you need to make lights-on decisions that will move you toward your vision, and ultimately toward living your life purpose, your destiny.

The question is, how can you stay in present time when your mind is drawn to the past and the future? Now that you have been in flow for a while, one effective way is to continually ask yourself the question, *What will it take right now to advance my vision?* Your answer can help you form a revised bridge plan. Remember: a bridge plan is a strategy that allows you to move from where you are now to where you want to be, while remaining energized, intentional, and clear. Bridge-planning is a dynamic, on-going process that recognizes when your original vision has morphed and you have moved on to Plan B, or C, or D. Actually, you could view a vision-led life as a series of bridge plans, as the river moves you from one spot to the next on your journey.

Only by being awake and aware in present time will you be able to spot important clues and life lessons as they appear, and see how to connect them. Awareness of what's happening in the moment allows you to experience synchronicity—the concurrence of events that are meaningfully related—and use that concurrence to your advantage. This is done by seeing how the clues and lessons that have appeared to you fit together to form a picture of your own unique expression, your contribution to the world.

Clarity in Action: Carla's Story

An example from a retreat several years ago points to the power of staying present and open to following the clues. Everyone in the retreat was an entrepreneur in different stages of building a business they were passionate about; several would also need funding to take their business to the level of their most expansive vision.

Also in this particular group of women business leaders was Carla who had recently divorced; as a result, she had significant financial resources available to her. Her reason for attending the retreat was to gain clarity about what she wanted to do with these resources. Before attending she had mentioned to Cathy that she was thinking of creating either a charitable foundation, investing in a family member's company or doing something that benefited women business owners. With all of these possibilities, she wanted to know where her energy was with respect to each of the options.

She spent several days in the retreat with this group of female entrepreneurs exploring passionate visions. Synchronicity happened. As a result of the connection formed during the week, Carla ultimately invested in one of the women's growing venture. As a result of following her own energy, she also invested in the family company. In addition, through her connections with *Clarity*, she ultimately met two other women who were building a real estate business and she invested in them as well.

It is fun to think of your life as a destiny jigsaw puzzle, with the clues as the puzzle pieces. So far on the journey you have sorted through all of the clues, and discarded such lights-off pieces as other people's advice and opinions and your own self-criticism, doubt, fear, and self-defeating patterns. The remaining pieces are your lights-on clues. Linked together, they form a clear picture of the destiny that is calling you forward. The closer you get to sailing home, you will remember that "home" means living your life on purpose. The *clarity amnesia* that started you on this journey has vanished.

Doors open, people appear and opportunities happen when you stay awake and watch for what does show up. Things related to your vision begin to happen very quickly. We call it the *whoosh effect*.

Clarity in Action: John's Story

John is a very successful commercial real estate broker. For many years his biggest vision was to become a developer, building his own office buildings. With coaching he began to build his bridge plan toward that vision. John had always had a special interest in environmental issues and one of his bridge steps was to learn more about green buildings.

During the following year as he pursued knowledge about green buildings, he began to notice that a few potential commercial tenants were expressing a desire for finding space in green buildings; this was a few years before it became part of the national conversation. After the third person asked the question, John took it as a big clue. He began to quicken and deepen his study. Ultimately, he became LEED certified (Leadership in Energy and Environmental Design).

Continuing on his bridge plan, John purchased his first small office building and did a complete green remodel, becoming the first green real estate developer in his state. He has since added more buildings to his inventory. His lights-on bridge strategy led him to his vision of being a commercial real estate developer even though his original vision did not include doing it green. He followed the clues, stayed present and continued to ask what he could do to serve his vision.

Clarity in Action: Sharon's Story

When Sharon started the *Get Clarity* retreat, she was ready to reinvent her life. She was vibrantly healthy, in her early fifties, and had put her two children through college. She was looking at the second half of her life as a blank book in which to write her future.

Knowing she could do anything she wanted, Sharon said, "This time it's for me! I'm ready to do life my way." Yet she wasn't clear about what that life would be. She felt an exhilarating sense of freedom: at the same time she was totally baffled about her direction. So she asked herself, *What will it take right now to create the clarity I need to advance my vision?*

Sharon realized that she needed a bridge plan to keep her in action until she became crystal clear about her future. Her job at a large software company would address her present needs, providing her with an income while she explored future possibilities. She had faith that if she could be clear about what she wanted and put that vision out into the universe, the universe would handle the details.

When Sharon was eighteen, her dream had been to combine spiritual life with psychology and the arts. In the visioning process, that dream reappeared, and she saw how to make it a reality. She decided to go to college full time and study to be a spiritual psychologist. She also decided to relocate to a warmer climate. She realized that to make all that happen as soon as possible, she would need to quit her job— and absorb the financial consequences of leaving before she was fully vested in her employer's retirement plan.

To concentrate fully on her schooling meant Sharon would need a plan that would allow her to live without an income for several years. The company stock was her only asset, and its value was at an all-time low. It seemed like an impossible dream. Monkey mind and shadow talk began an intense conversation, telling her she was crazy to be dreaming like this. Her mind conjured up a worst-case scenario in which she ended up on the street destitute, a bag lady.

Fortunately, she had received enough coaching to shift her attention from doubt and worry to her destiny—a best-case scenario. This shift of attention broke the pattern of going around in circles in her mind, unable to go into action. With her vision clear, Sharon started to gather information about spiritual psychology programs. In addition to assembling factual information, she also stayed alert to clues and synchronicity. She called this, "Being open to guidance."

Since part of her vision was to live in a cottage in a warmer climate, she decided to investigate possibilities in a city she loved—Santa Fe, New Mexico. Before she even had time to visit Santa Fe, her sister called out of the blue, offering Sharon a house-sitting position rent free. Her sister's rental house had just been vacated, and she wanted a trustworthy person to live there and supervise a remodel. Not only was the house located in southern California—a warmer climate, just as Sharon had envisioned—but it was on Santa Fe Street!

When Sharon put together all the clues—free rent, a cottage on Santa Fe Street, a nearby university offering her desired program—she felt truly guided. The synchronicity told her that the timing was right for her to go into action.

Over the next two years, while completing her education, Sharon enjoyed being able to live frugally without an income. Since graduation, she has lived out the rest of her dream—working with abused children using expressive arts therapy.

Navigational Tools: Staying Present

Using all of the *Clarity* tools—vision mapping, check-in, ritual, holding your energy, Clarity Attention Guides and others—everyday will help you stay present and allow you to make effective daily decisions; form clarity for the next steps; and create the appropriate long term strategies.

- At a minimum, ask yourself often "What worked" and "What didn't work" in your performance. Remember: remove judgment and criticism.

- Make a list of patterns that you need to be aware of and be especially watchful for.

- Watch for clues and synchronous events. Stay curious. Review the past three months, make note of any clues that appeared to provide you with something you needed.

- Stay objective; don't take any information personally.

- Create a new bridge plan and add more lights-on action steps. Bridge plans are dynamic. They need to be modified frequently, as flow moves you to a new spot on the journey. Place some action steps on the bridge that are energizing and will move you closer to your goal.

Chapter Fifteen

Refreshing Your Vision

*Revealing and realizing Noble Purpose is about returning
to that which is most essential within you, discovering
your perfect wisdom, fulfilling that which seeks expression
within you. The journey to Noble Purpose is essentially
awakening from your deep sleep to this inner call.*
—Dr. Barry Heermann, Author and Educator

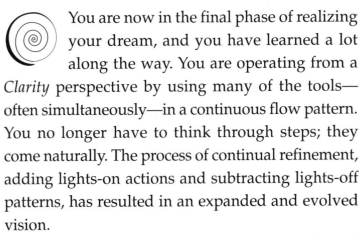 You are now in the final phase of realizing
your dream, and you have learned a lot
along the way. You are operating from a
Clarity perspective by using many of the tools—
often simultaneously—in a continuous flow pattern.
You no longer have to think through steps; they
come naturally. The process of continual refinement,
adding lights-on actions and subtracting lights-off
patterns, has resulted in an expanded and evolved
vision.

When you find yourself stuck momentarily and
unable to move forward, you have learned to switch

your strategy, adjusting timing or financing or anything else involved in making your dream a reality.

At this point in your journey, you can truly appreciate the wisdom of the saying, "Life is what
happens when you're making other plans"—and as
often as not, it's Plan B. Dreams that are passionate
and connected to your heart take on a life of their
own as you continually refine them to keep them
viable.

It is obvious by now that some self reflection is
necessary to create a life of peak experiences; self-
reflection that does require taking the time from your
daily activities. It can merely be a time out for a few
minutes during your daily routine, an hour away
from the office or an actual retreat for a few days.

Doing any of these will allow you to reevaluate
and refresh your vision and help you discover the
strategies needed to align your actions. Taking the
time to retreat and refresh is actually being action
oriented—it helps you take vision-aligned action.

Taking a longer reflective break every year to
refresh your vision is another important tool for full
expression of your life. One of the most grounded
men we know is our friend, Barry. His way of staying
centered is to treat himself to five days every quarter
in a solitude experience. He has done this for over
two decades.

We realize that taking twenty days a year to retreat
and reflect is a treat you may not want or cannot

have. However, taking an extended period of time every year to reflect on your life and work will return incredible benefits. Barry has used the learning he's gained from his retreats to write two incredible books and develop an international group of highly committed trainers.

Clarity in Action: Gerri's Story

Gerri has a very successful business selling real estate. Her success is a direct result of the time and individual attention she spends on each client. More than just a real estate agent, she helps people find their ideal living space and handles all the details involved in making their dreams come true. Her clients love her, and she loves her work.

In addition to real estate matchmaking, Gerri has another love, which she discovered during a shamanic retreat: protecting the endangered sea turtle. From the moment she awakened to the plight of the sea turtles, helping them has become her calling. Her deep desire is to give a gift to the planet: that gift is to use her time and real estate profits to establish a sea turtle sanctuary on an island somewhere in the Caribbean. Gerri's vision is that the property will contain both the sanctuary and a retreat center for eco-tourism.

To put her vision into action, Gerri and her husband took a sabbatical and traveled through the Caribbean on a sailboat, looking for an island. They chose to travel under sail in order to have the same vantage point as a turtle searching for a place to land and lay her eggs.

The trip proved to be magical. Many sea turtles came right up alongside their boat. One turtle in particular stood out and reappeared often: the captain of their boat said it was the largest, and therefore the oldest, turtle he had seen in all his years sailing those waters. Gerri came to believe that the turtle was her totem—her spirit guide from the animal kingdom.

During those weeks in the Caribbean, Gerri and her husband stopped at several ports and investigated available real estate. They explored extensively but found nothing that met Gerri's vision. Fortunately, her belief system that "everything is perfect as it is" kept them from being discouraged. They released their original intention to purchase land on that trip and returned home with the knowledge that more time and money would be necessary to find the right property.

Meanwhile, to raise more money for the turtle sanctuary, Gerri revised her strategy, adjusting for the changes in her original timeline and financial plans. She focused on manifesting a new real estate project capable of rapidly producing income. Setting her intention, she called on all her developer contacts and within weeks, landed a contract to sell 102 new homes. She sold out the entire project in just three months.

Gerri's search for the perfect Caribbean location continues. But her success to date demonstrates that when you energetically create a strategy to compensate for changes you've encountered, you will be rewarded with rapid confirmation that "Plan B" is still an excellent choice.

Navigational Tools: Refresh and Refine Your Vision

Whether you take a week, a day or even a few hours every year, it is important to use the time to reflect on what you have achieved toward your vision and set your intention for the coming year. One approach to a reflective retreat that we find to be very effective is to do an annual version of the Clarity daily check-in. If you do this every year, you will be energized by how much has been accomplished when you review your old notes.

- What's different in the past year? What did you achieve towards your vision? What aligned actions have you taken? Acknowledge all that you have accomplished on your leadership journey.

- What worked in the past year in your performance? Be sure to fully acknowledge and appreciate all that you did to improve your performance. Look back at all of the principles you incorporated into your way of being every day. Make a list of all of your actions, thoughts and behaviors that worked. This is a time to acknowledge your performance and celebrate your accomplishments.

- What could you have done differently to be more effective? As you know, this is not a place for self judgment or criticism. Merely list the facts of your year's performance and what could have been done more effectively. What are some strategies you can incorporate into your daily life to address these less effective behaviors in the coming year?

- What is the state of your mind? At this time of annual reflection, what is the state of your mind? Is your mind clear, open, and anticipating the wonder and possibilities of the year to come?

- What is the state of your body? Are you physically comfortable? Are you healthy and fit? Are there areas of stress or discomfort that you need to create strategies to address in the coming year?

- What is the state of your spirit as you approach the next year? Is it light, grateful, expansive, or creative? Let your intuition and your intention access the state of your spirit as you envision what you want for the coming year.

- What are you grateful for? What has happened in the past year that fills you with gratitude at this reflective moment in time? Who are the people who have enriched your experiences this year? Do you have gratitude for all the lessons you have learned this year? Do you feel gratitude for the abundance and flow you have experienced? Is there gratitude for the opportunities you have as this new year begins?

- What is your intention? What are your most expansive intentions for the coming year? Where do you want to put your focus and your aligned actions? Where can you be the most effective to achieving your vision?

- Create a new vision map. This annual check-in will help you refine and refresh your vision. Look at all that you have noted and make a list of anything that can be added to your expanding vision. What do you want to add to your most expansive desires for your work and your life? Add these to your new vision map.

Chapter Sixteen
Plunging into Your Destiny

You must give birth to your images. They are the future
waiting to be born. Fear not the strangeness that you feel.
The future must enter you long before it happens.
Just wait for the hour, the birth of new clarity.
—Rainer Maria Rilke, German Poet

Everything is perfect, and as it should be—that is our belief. But sometimes what shows up initially may not look perfect to you at the time. However, by releasing the outcome—your willful picture of how you think it should look—you allow for serendipity to provide your perfect solution. Once you have successfully let go of your attachment to a certain outcome you will be able to say, "I was clear about my intention, and what showed up is perfect."

There is a formula to follow for getting what you want and manifesting your dream. It involves using all the tools you have learned on your *Clarity* journey: *Intention + Attention + Action + Release the Outcome = Manifestation of Your Vision.*

Intention: You set your intention having a clear, lights-on vision for what you want. You write down your vision, stating fully what you want—not what you don't want. It is also important to have a visual representation of your vision to remind you often of what you want: vision maps, lists of lights-on clues, and bridge plans are all part of setting your intention.

Attention: You focus your attention on creating your vision. What you focus on expands, gaining more and more of your attention, so you need to focus only on what you want. Allow yourself time to visualize often what you want to create. Using rapid discovery and rapid recovery will help you keep your attention on what you are creating.

Action: You step directly into action that is aligned with your vision, following the lights-on action steps on your bridge plan. The action steps must energize you, so that your experience as an energy detective will help you discern which action steps to take yourself and which ones to delegate to others. Watch for clues: Is there effort involved in what you're doing, or does it flow easily? *High noticing* and observing resistance will serve you well here.

Release the outcome: Putting all your energy into forcing the results you want will keep you from seeing a better version of your dream if that's what appears. Practice the mantra: "I was clear about my intention, and what showed up is perfect"—whatever it is.

Manifestation of your vision: When you hold your personal energy field and don't revert to old patterns, vision-to-outcome happens rapidly. In *Clarity* terms, the very short time gap between envisioning an outcome and its actual occurrence is known as the "whoosh effect." In some cases, the result is instantaneous. So fasten your seat belt and be very clear about what you ask for!

Clarity in Action: Gary's Story

At age 57, Gary was at a major choice point: what he wanted most was to find a life partner, someone with whom he could connect on all levels—body, mind, and spirit. He felt as if he had been searching his whole life for this elusive person, never finding exactly what he was looking for. He valued committed relationships and family ties—he had been married previously and had a wonderful son—but still, he was unfulfilled. After being divorced for a few years, he had a deep desire to find his soul mate.

In searching for a partner, Gary felt compelled to do things differently than he had in the past and to be more conscious and decisive. His previous pattern had been to romanticize his partner and ignore any signs that didn't match this image. Overriding

his instincts, he would settle for a less than lights-
on relationship, and then feel guilty and not fully
committed when it proved unfulfilling. He was determined to break his pattern of inability to commit
and compromise. This time he was going to choose
passion over pattern, no matter what!

After a few years of searching, he realized that he
still hadn't kicked the old pattern. He was still com-
promising and dissatisfied. Gary began to experience
doubt. His monkey mind caused him to question if
he really could do partnership differently. He made
a conscious decision to stop dating for a year and
spend time gaining clarity about himself. He hired
a coach and began a process of self-discovery and
creating a new vision.

Gary's coach assigned him the task of writing
down a description of his ideal partner—a profile
of the woman he wanted in his life. Gary was very
specific about the qualities he was looking for. Once
again, however, doubt assailed him, and he wondered
if he was the man who could attract the woman he
described.

At his coach's urging Gary then drafted a description of the man he truly was, not the man
his monkey mind described. At the same time, he
defined more clearly the woman he was seeking.
This process of continual refinement allowed him to
look closely at who he truly was as well as who he

wanted to attract. Finally, he arrived at a refreshed vision that was very compelling.

With renewed excitement and intention, Gary began dating again with the specific purpose of finding his true life partner. Over the next year he met a number of interesting and amazing women. However, by staying committed to his vision, he didn't follow his previous pattern of settling for a woman who seemed likely but was not the one he had envisioned.

Synchronicity began to operate almost immediately after Gary decided to renew his search. He and a good friend took a road trip to experience a solitude retreat in Northern California. During his time of solitude, Gary reviewed the list of qualities and characteristics he had drawn up a few weeks earlier and created a more detailed profile of the woman he wanted to meet. On the return trip home, he shared the profile with his friend.

A few months later, the friend called and told Gary that he knew someone who fit the profile perfectly. When Gary found out that this woman lived 1,800 miles away, he said thanks, but he wasn't interested in long-distance dating. Several times over the next seven or eight months, the friend suggested ways for Gary to meet this woman. He even sent Gary a message that began, "I figure that part of my purpose on being on this earth is to support you in finding your passion around a wonderful woman." Gary finally got the message. He let go of his objection to a long-distance relationship and called the mystery woman.

After a few weeks of exhilarating and enlightening phone conversations, they agreed to meet. Right away, Gary knew he had found his soul mate. A month later, they decided to get married. Today, Gary and Cathy are co-creative partners in both their personal and professional lives.

Two years after they were married, Gary received another lesson in how releasing the outcome can allow you to experience an even better version of your dream. Going through some old files, he found a document entitled "My Ideal Scene." It was a vision for his life that he had written five years earlier. What he had envisioned at the time included spending half of his time writing creatively and publishing a novel about an entrepreneur. He had also written, "My primary work is writing on the issues I hold in my heart, and conducting workshops in the areas of leadership and self-discovery."

As he read that document, Gary's first reaction was disappointment that he hadn't achieved his ideal. The novel hadn't been written, and the organization he envisioned to do leadership workshops had never fully materialized. However, he quickly recognized all the things that *had* shown up in response to his original vision.

Since meeting Cathy, he has spent much of his time co-authoring a book and several workshop manuals with her, including one on using the *Clarity* process to create lights-on leadership in organizations; writing blogs, newsletters, and marketing materials for their company, Clarity International; conducting *Get Clarity* retreats with Cathy; and facilitating several peer groups of business owners who want to grow as leaders.

By looking at what had actually shown up, it was obvious to Gary that his life and work provided the same joyful energy that had animated his original vision. He is truly living the life he dreamed of. A few of the details are different, but the core essence of his vision is magnificently present.

One aspect of Gary's original five-year-old vision did show up exactly as written: "I am in a great, loving relationship with a woman of character, passion, wit, feminine essence, and grace." Now he's fully able to endorse the last sentence of his original vision: "And the rest of my life is perfect as well."

Once you make a conscious, vision-supported decision, and you pay attention and step energetically into action, you will see results very quickly.

Navigational Tools: Be Clear

Gary's story perfectly illustrates the benefits of being very clear about your intentions in all aspects of your vision.

- Keep your focus fully engaged on what you want and stay conscious of where your thoughts are.

- Step into aligned action immediately and be observant of the energy flow.

- Release the outcome and joyfully watch what shows up in response to your intention.

- Notice how quickly your vision manifests. Often, it happens as soon as you think it. If you are still unclear what role synchronicity can play in manifesting your vision, keep track of "coincidences" as they occur in your life. Note how the concurrence of a dream or thought or feeling with an external event moves you in the direction of your vision.

- Hold on to your hat and relish the rapid acceleration of the whoosh effect!

Chapter Seventeen
Living Lights-On

*You are what your deep driving desire is. As your desire is,
so is your will. As your will is, so is your deed.
As your deed is, so is your destiny.*
—Upanishads, ancient Indian text

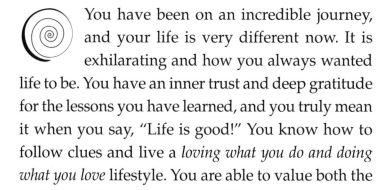 You have been on an incredible journey, and your life is very different now. It is exhilarating and how you always wanted life to be. You have an inner trust and deep gratitude for the lessons you have learned, and you truly mean it when you say, "Life is good!" You know how to follow clues and live a *loving what you do and doing what you love* lifestyle. You are able to value both the peaks and the valleys of your life.

Events that earlier in the *Clarity* journey might have seemed catastrophic—divorce, death of a loved one, illness or injury, job loss—now appear as opportunities for re-visioning, learning, and growth. Regardless of what happens, you are able to continue on your lights-on path. There is no going back and living your life the old way. Going forward, your journey is illuminated and purposeful.

On the *Get Clarity* map, you will see that by now you have parked your boat, symbolizing the end of that phase of your journey. You no longer need the boat to carry you along in the flow. This ending marks a new beginning. Your feet are on the ground, and your back pack is filled with heart-connected wisdom and energy tools to keep you on the path. You have "cracked the clarity code" by learning that you must always use your heart energy, not just the power of your intellect, to guide you. Old thinking patterns have dissolved. Overanalyzing, without also observing your energy, no longer serves you. Your vision is linked to passion, and it produces a powerful chain reaction of energy—an acceleration effect. You can feel when that heart connection occurs.

As you come to this phase of the *Clarity* journey, manifestation is rapid. You envision something and it shows up. In honoring your own distinct energy patterns, you know that you are following guidance instead of your will. Your energy remains constant, and you are able to stay lights-on. There is a noticeable increase in your vitality and, simultaneously, a feeling of ease and peace. People who meditate call it "restful awareness," and you live your life in that state every day.

You have left behind your old, indecisive ways. At choice points you choose intentionally and create clear outcomes. No more accidental bumping into life. Your journey forward is transformed with passion and purpose.

There are so many more stories of transformation that we can tell you, and we wish we had room to tell them all. They are stories of everyday heroes and heroines who have courageously faced coming undone and then reforming in a new and more passionate way, to live their dreams: an architect who became a country music composer; a real estate developer who became an expert in overseas relocations; a PhD scientist who became a blues singer; a concierge who became a seminar leader; a financial advisor who became an internet marketing advisor; a nutritionist who became an equine-assisted therapist; a bookseller who became a retreat-center owner.

And there are just as many stories of people who used the *Clarity* journey to refresh their visions and revitalize their energy: a business owner who found a new love for her company rather than sell it; a couple on the verge of divorce who found loving power in holding their own energy; a therapist who gained a new connection with her patients; a seminar speaker who found a renewed voice. Like the people whose stories we included in the book, they've made the changes you dream of.

They are people who are now living each day, happily free of judgment or criticism. They continue to create their reality by making daily choices that are lights-on and choosing energizing actions that move them forward. They are attracting what they want into their life energetically and focusing their attention on manifesting magnificent lives. They look younger and brighter, feel healthier, and love what they're doing. That, in short, is the definition of lights-on living.

When you started this journey, the river seemed long, and the prospect overwhelming. Now that you have arrived at the end, scaled the mountain, and are looking down, the river seems less formidable, and you are grateful it has carried you along to safety. From this vantage point, it is easy to see the rewards of making this heroic journey: remembrance of your destiny and calling; an embodied process in which you have learned to create new visions and strategies; and the knowledge to sustain the journey through the peaks and valleys as your life continues to unfold.

As the poet T.S. Eliot wrote, "To make an end is to make a beginning. The end is where we start from."

Appendix 1
Peer Coaching

Peer coaching is a very valuable exercise to expand the energetic feedback. This clear feedback you will receive, will deepen your awareness of the energy in your mind and body. This process also expands your team of strategic allies; you can be mutually supportive as you create envisioned lives.

Peer coaching begins with gathering two friends who are curious and interested in finding some clues about energy, thus forming a feedback group. When choosing your feedback group, it is important to choose people who are willing to suspend projection of what they think you should do—to refrain from judgment, criticism, opinions, or advice. Be sure to screen carefully, as most people want to give "friendly advice." And, although well-meaning, they often use their own fear and worry to "protect" you, which keeps you from clearly articulating your vision. We call the feedback group "strategic allies" because they are excellent observers. They can listen with curiosity and look for your lights-on energy without any preconceived notions.

Once you have assembled your allies, allow ninety minutes to complete the process.

Peer coaching involves three roles: *the client* (the person being coached), *the coach*, and the *scribe*. Each person will spend thirty minutes in each role, learning the skills associated with each position. The scribe will gain skills of deep listening, the coach will practice pure curiosity, and the client will learn to answer questions as if anything is possible. At the end of the process, all three of you will have your own list of lights-on clues.

Seat yourselves comfortably in a triad, making sure that it is easy to see and hear one another. Each person picks a starting role. Note the time. The coach will begin the interview with the "Santa Claus" question, the client will answer, and the scribe will take notes of lights-on responses only, using the client's own words. Spend twenty-five minutes interviewing, then have the scribe read back the notes for five minutes. After thirty minutes, switch roles. Repeat this process until you have each experienced all three roles.

The "Santa Claus" question is asked like this: *"If I were Santa Claus and could give you anything you wanted, what would that be?"* To avoid leading the client, it is important to start with this wide open question. When the client answers, look for what lights the person up as a starting point and continue your questioning by following their lights-on energy. If the coach remains dedicated to staying neutral and curious and observing, the clues to lights-on energy will be apparent. Make sure the scribe records the client's lights-on responses verbatim without elaborating or editorializing.

Expect conceptual answers from the client such as wanting freedom or peace, and then ask what that looks like. Stay curious and continue questioning until specifics and clarity emerge.

If the answer is "I want everything," ask what everything looks like. It is important for the client to be focused. If the answer is "I don't know," just continue to stay curious and playful, and ask the "Santa Claus" question again.

The client will then use the scribe's notes of the lights-on clues as a guide in the first step of the Get Clarity© Journey Map.

Peer Coaching Guidelines

While in the role of coach, follow these guidelines:

- Never ask why. Why requires justification. Stay with who, what, where, when questions.

- Brainstorm with care. It can become thinly disguised advising. Advising sounds like:

    "You should..."
    "I think..."
    "That won't work..."
    "Well, if you want my opinion..."
    "You know, what would be good is..."

- Move quickly out of any storytelling by the client, and go to solution. Storytelling occurs when the client tries to explain why things are the way they are, or why something can't be done. It keeps the focus on the past and doesn't provide energetic clues. Guide the client into saying what he/she wants, not talking about what he/she doesn't want.

- Hold your own energy field by staying curious and observant.

Peer Coaching Triad

Procedure
(Switch roles every 30 minutes)

General Peer Coaching Guidelines
No nodding. Hold a still field.
No agreement. Stay curious.

Client
Answers as if anything is possible!

Coach

Asks questions.

Uses interview guidelines.

Uses "Santa Claus" questions from the client's area of focus.

Follows lights-on.

Acts as a High Noticer.

Scribe

Scribes what lights client up.

Refrains from talking.

Acts as a Deep Listener.

Reads lights-on list back with no editorializing.

Appendix 2
Get Clarity for Leaders

Inspire a Shared Vision,
Create a Lights-On Culture

*Perhaps the most distinguishing trait of visionary leaders is
that they believe in a goal that benefits not only themselves,
but others as well. It is such vision that attracts the
psychic energy of other people, and makes them willing
to work beyond the call of duty for the organization.*
—Mihaly Csikszentmihalyi, Professor and Author

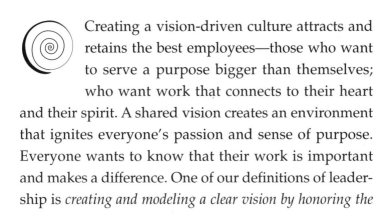 Creating a vision-driven culture attracts and
retains the best employees—those who want
to serve a purpose bigger than themselves;
who want work that connects to their heart
and their spirit. A shared vision creates an environment
that ignites everyone's passion and sense of purpose.
Everyone wants to know that their work is important
and makes a difference. One of our definitions of leadership is *creating and modeling a clear vision by honoring the*

individual spirit, by igniting passion and purpose and creating flow between individual spirit and organizational vision. This is leading with *Clarity.*

As a leader, the process of bringing this spirit into your organization or your team begins with you. It all begins with your vision of what you want to create. Without your own vision being deeply and passionately connected to the work you do, it is almost impossible to awaken the passions and productivity of the people you work with.

You may have had the experience of working as part of a team where everything clicked. It just felt right. Everyone worked together with flow and ease. The feeling was incredible and energizing. Coming to work was pure joy; knowing you were part of something bigger than you. There was a purpose to your work. The people you worked with were your friends and the work you did together made a difference.

Certainly there were challenges. But, all the team members wanted to be there, and gave the work, the project, the team their best stuff. There was an aliveness to the place that was palpable. Everyone who came in contact with that energy noticed it and wanted to be part of the aliveness.

Most people yearn to be part of an organization that provides this experience. It's not just about having a good job and a good paycheck. It's about the daily work experience that connects to their heart and spirit. They want work that energizes and enriches their very soul. They want a work environment that ignites their passion and purpose by giving them a vision to be inspired by, and an environment that supports that shared vision every day. That's the "wow" of employee experience. As the leader, you can create the environment that ignites that passion and purpose by giving them a vision that inspires them.

In the early 90s Gary worked for a rapidly growing weight-loss services company. Working there during that time was an opportunity to experience the awesome power of shared vision in action. Everyone in that company shared in the vision of providing the highest quality weight-loss services in a caring manner to each client. We knew our services were the best and we cared the most. As soon as a new employee was hired, the indoctrination on the vision and mission of the company began and considerable time was spent training each employee so that she would have a shared vision with the rest of us.

Clarity in Action: Sam's story

Cathy coached Sam, founder of a very successful manufacturing company, who had a very clear vision about what he wanted to happen with his company. He was totally committed to having his son and daughter take over, and had spent several years mentoring and grooming them to be successful.

However, he also sent out confusing signals to them and to the several hundred employees of the company. Because the company was so successful, Sam was periodically courted by much larger companies seeking to purchase his company. Sam enjoyed the attention and a couple of times invited the "suitors" in to see what they thought the company was worth. In his mind, he wasn't modifying his vision, but only flirting with admirers. However, what others perceived was that he was truly interested in selling to outsiders, if the money was right.

Cathy asked him whether he was communicating his vision to his successors and employees. Sam said, "They all know what my vision is. I've told them." He did tell his children once in a while, but not that often. When they watched him taking an opposite action, it confused them. He failed to explain clearly his motivation.

Following Cathy's coaching, Sam began a campaign of telling everyone in company gatherings, family dinners, private conversations that he had no intention of selling the company, that it was going to continue under the leadership of his chosen and trained successors. At the first public employee meeting where he clearly shared this vision, the relief flowing through the employees was palpable. An interesting, and not unexpected, result was increased production in the months following his focused declarations.

A common business owner's lament is, "How do I motivate my employees?" It is our belief that the word "motivate" should be stricken from your vocabulary.

We believe the question should be, "How do I inspire my employees?" This puts the focus on the most powerful tool for developing the employee actions you want—their individual spirit.

Motivation is an external force that seldom has a lasting impact. Inspiration is more of an individual, inside job that connects with each employee at a deeper, more lasting and effective level. At the heart of inspiration is "spirit." Connecting with the spirit of each of your employees requires connecting your vision to their individual vision and purpose. Then they also will have reasons to get up in the morning and be part of creating something with a bigger purpose.

In *First, Break All The Rules,* Marcus Buckingham and Curt Coffman wrote about the Gallup Organization's study of what great managers do differently. They discovered that the strength of an organization can be measured by twelve core elements needed to attract, focus, and keep the most talented employees. One of these key twelve is, "Does the mission/purpose of my company make me feel like my work is important?"

If you are taking the time to hire the right people, it is imperative that you also take the time to make sure you know what's important to them and what they are passionate about. Good employees come into a new job wanting to make a contribution, and may already be forming ideas of how their vision for their life is complimented by this particular company and job. It is critical to assist them in making the connection early and often.

Clarity in Action: Greg's story

Our friend, Greg, is an example of the kind of employee any company would love to have. He always wants to perform at his highest level. We've watched him over several years, and he has been successful in four separate and distinct industries—corporate computer sales, video production, distribution of industrial parts, and optical lens manufacturing.

Greg's often voiced desire is to do quality work that makes a real contribution to the world while making a good living to support his family. His desire was evident in our conversations before he began each of his new jobs. He could instantly see and describe in detail how this particular company and its services made a difference in the world, even when he hadn't worked in the industry before. He began voicing this belief even before he walked in the door for his first day on the job.

His own internal guiding vision helped him be very productive in his new work. He spread his enthusiasm to other employees and customers. He constantly talked about how important the company's work is to the world. And, he saw his place in the whole scheme.

Then a shift happened, and Greg ultimately moved on to another employer. In each case, the shift was a direct result of his boss, the company owner, not having a strong vision or creating an atmosphere that was totally opposite to the stated vision that Greg so wanted to be part of. So, Greg moved on with his yearning to find the one place where he can happily work with others in a shared purpose that contributes to the larger good. Fortunately, Greg is now working for someone who leads from vision every day.

It's critically important to understand that everyone wants to be connected to a purposeful vision. They may not have experienced it in past employment. They may not fully know what they are passionate about or what their own purpose is, but they all have a yearning for it. That yearning will help them connect with and share your vision.

Clarity in Action: Harold's story

A former client, Harold, is a fine furniture manufacturer. His company now has over 300 employees and does about $40 million in revenue. One of his stories is that his original vision was to be an artist building fine furniture one piece at a time with his own hands. He says he even took a vow of poverty so he could be an example of dedication to his art.

At some point he began to hire craftsmen to help him. When the company reached sales of $1 million with half a dozen craftsmen, Harold tried to walk away—give it to his employees—and return to his art. They wouldn't let him go. They wanted and needed his ability to state a clear vision of fine furniture being in homes and offices throughout the country. He repeats this story often to show the power of an enduring vision.

It is critical to bring the shared vision alive and current into the daily work. To create a culture of shared purpose and vision, you need to personally model and exhibit the behaviors. And, tell stories often about the people and their actions that support the shared vision. Be dramatic.

The craftsmen in Harold's company seldom get to see their work in its final form inside the offices and homes. To help them connect their work with the beauty of its final setting, Harold, being an artist at heart, brings photographs to his craftsman. These photographs are mounted in quality frames along a hall of pride where every day the craftsman can see their work and know they make a difference in their customers' lives. Harold also often shares the customers' comments and excitement they experience from working in and living with the fine woodwork the craftsmen created.

Share the vision often; make it real to people. Some will join you because they also have a vision that dovetails with yours. Others are searching or yearning for one and will latch on to yours, and see it as shared.

Navigation Tools:
Create a Shared Vision

Take the time to conduct an employee retreat with the total focus on developing a shared vision. Give each person opportunity to fully express his or her big vision for their life and for the company. While many leaders hesitate to take time away from the office for events like this, we know it is a critical piece for creating a powerful team connection, individual responsibility and a shared desire to achieve the common purpose. Don't short change the process with fear of losing productive work time. Doing this process with enthusiasm and commitment will more than make up for any loss of production that may result from a day or two away from the office.

You may want to bring in a trained facilitator that is familiar with following the lights-on clues of everyone involved and creating an energetic atmosphere of open conversation. It's important that this retreat be focused on energetic exchange regarding everyone's expansive vision and should not get bogged down in the how-to's of the work or the action steps that will be required. The appropriate actions steps will become more clear when the shared vision is fully developed.

Among retreat objectives should be:

- A vision discovery process that many companies find helpful is using *Peer Coaching*. *Peer Coaching* is a very valuable exercise because it expands the energetic feedback so each person and the group as a whole gain more information on what lights everyone up. The process of using pure energetic feedback deepens the awareness of everyone's energy and passions. Use the peer coaching triads discussed in the *Peer Coaching* Appendix to conduct the interviews and then have each employee create their own individual Vision Map. Then as a group create a shared vision using the common elements of each of the individual visions.

- Create a *Shared Vision Map* that will visually remind everyone of your common purpose. When you return to the office, place the *Shared Vision Map* in a prominent place where everyone can see it, and refer to it often.

- Be open and accepting of the chaos that happens before the shared vision is created. Allow the energy to flow through the chaos by watching for everyone's lights-on energy. Chaos is a critical part of any creation and it can be uncomfortable for many, especially people used to action and instant results. Experiencing the chaos is also a necessary part of the process.

- While your vision as the leader is integral to the development of a shared vision, don't let the retreat be only about getting everyone on board with your vision. Allow the energetic flow of all visions to add detail and richness that comes from everyone being involved with its development.

Having a vision map that everyone can easily see, gives life to the words and helps connect to the passion behind the words. It helps everyone see their thinking; engaging everyone's right brain. Having a visual representation of a vision is a critical part of human cognition. Quoting Dan Roam, *The Back of the Napkin: Solving Problems and Selling Ideas with Pictures*:

Between information overload, globalization, and the sheer complexity of modern business, we've got to be more visual and less language dependent in communicating ideas.

A shared visioning retreat is a very inspiring, powerful and energizing activity. One of our leader clients had this to say after conducting his first retreat with his staff:

> *I held a staff retreat for my leadership team. For the first time I explained my vision for the company—very powerful. I showed my own personal vision map and I was amazed at how powerful a presentation it was. Each staff person created and presented their visions and it was truly a touching moment. The best bonding of any activity we have ever done. I forgot how much I enjoy the selling of the dream and how excited I get talking about it. Second, I really forgot how much my employees need a constant reminder of what the dream is.*

Sharing your vision is one of the most important elements of your leadership role. For example:

- When interviewing new employees find out what they are passionate about. Make looking for lights and high noticing an integral part of your interviewing process. Ask them to describe their vision for what they want in their life and work. Watch for what lights them up. When they come on board as a new employee, educate and connect them to the company's shared vision from the moment they walk in the door.

- Share your vision often through stories, actions, and behaviors. Make this a part of your leadership every day. Be alert to the daily behaviors and actions of others that serve the shared vision. Point these out to the whole organization as examples of what you all do together to serve the organization's vision and purpose. Publically celebrate small and large actions that support and serve the larger shared vision.

- Don't stop here. Continue to refresh the vision with everyone.

Create a Lights-On Culture

Our invitation is that you help every single employee in your organization or team live and work by the *Get Clarity Visioning and Operating System*. The concepts apply and will work for every single person who works with you. Whether or not they lead others, the principles will help them become more effective self leaders. The energy they send and reflect in the workplace will help you create a lights-on culture.

Every company has a culture, whether created intentionally or not. Culture means having common traits, behaviors and patterns that tie people together. The goal of most leaders is to create a culture that is energizing, productive and effective where the employees are committed and engaged. Holding your own energy field is a primary requirement for achieving your vision for the organization, and it requires you to fully use the principles of *Get Clarity.* Creating a reflective space for everyone in your near field to achieve the shared vision requires that they also use the system.

The operating system we present to you here will create a way for everyone to operate with the same language, approach, behaviors and intentions. It will foster the enthusiasm, energy and commitment you want in your organization. *Get Clarity* creates a culture of vision, engagement, integrity, energetic connection and effective behaviors.

Teach it. Invest the time to train everyone. To reach the shared vision you have created together, it is also imperative that you all live the shared principles so you can stay in aligned action to achieve it. Doing this will energize and engage everyone.

Gary worked with a company that invested annually in having many of its 400 employees participate in 360 degree assessments and feedback. His role was limited to providing individual, 360 degree feedback reports to several people at different levels of the organization—Vice President to individual contributors—one of whom— Megan—had a team of four people reporting to her.

During Megan's coaching with Gary she began to connect with her own vision which included bringing some new energetic principles into her work. During her next meeting with her direct reports, she opened by asking them to say their vision for what they wanted from work as well as their vision for what they wanted for the team. She was met with blank stares. "They looked at me like I was nuts."

Having no experience in creating a shared vision with her team, she intuitively kept asking questions to see where their energy was. Over the next few meetings, she kept the dialogue going. Then Megan began to notice something. All the members of her staff began to show more enthusiasm in the way they approached their daily work and how they related to each other. She said the difference was apparent to everyone, and it had begun after only a couple of sessions of asking vision questions and setting her intention to bring new energy into the team.

Clarity in Action: Sandra's story

Another client, Sandra, is founder of a regional business services company. After attending a *Get Clarity* retreat, she returned to her company and focused on bringing all the principles into the organization, at every level.

She began by using the peer coaching exercise with every employee to begin the process of visioning. Next, she required that every quarter each employee participate in a peer coaching triad to refresh their vision and enhance their whole-brain thinking skills. Each employee was paired with a co-worker to do the daily check-in and the *Clarity Attention Guide and Balance Sheet* was displayed prominently in the conference room to remind everyone of the behaviors that lead to effective performance. The change in employee engagement was apparent from the beginning and continues. And, they have an underlying system for more effectively handling the usual challenges of human interaction in the workplace.

Navigational Tools:
Live, Work and Lead with *Clarity*

Working with business leaders every day, we are well aware of the intensity and complexity of the typical workplace—a daily series of meetings; intense deadlines, and very little extra time to devote to training on human behavior or adding any daily rituals to the meetings.

From experience we also know that vision-led people who are passionate about their work, who pay attention to their impact on others, and who understand what energizes them and others, can reduce a lot of time spent with energy draining drama. We think this new understanding will more than make up for the time spent making *Clarity* a way of being in your workplace. Plus, it doesn't take that much time to learn and use the simple tools.

- Take the time to instill these principles in your organization through retreats, on-going trainings and daily usage. Make them part of your company's value system; use the language to encourage the effective, connecting behaviors that the language represents: "set your intention"; "hold your own field"; "apply high noticing"; "be an observer"; "stay awake"; "rapid discovery, rapid recovery"; "watch for your shadow"; "stay above the line."

- Hold frequent shared visioning retreats with your staff; teach the principles of *Get Clarity*. Walk the talk and do the daily check-in and other intention setting rituals frequently with employees.

- Place the shared vision map and the *Clarity Attention Guide and Balance Sheet* in prominent locations where everyone can be reminded of vision and effective behaviors. Give each employee an individual copy of the vision map and the *Guides*.

- Walk the talk and talk the talk. Use the language of energy every day. Create a team of *Clarity* champions who will keep the intention and the principles alive in the organization.

Glossary

Above the Line: A way of being that is energetically more effective, consisting of thoughts and behaviors that help you shift your attention and focus to making choices that are energizing, passionate, and solution-focused.

Biofield, or Energy Field: A matrix of energies that extends outward from the body and interacts with the energy fields of other people and the environment, providing a constant exchange and feedback of information.

Bridge Plan: A strategy with actions designed to move you from where you are now to where you want to go.

Cellular Learning: Learning that takes place internally, at a deep, physiological level.

Choice Point: A key moment on the *Clarity* journey when two or more divergent channels appear, offering an opportunity to make a decision that is energizing or draining.

Energy: An invisible force or current. In the body, it is the force of vitality, also known as life force, *chi, ki, prana,* and *élan vital.*

Energy Language: A metaphorical vernacular used to describe life force as it is seen and sensed. On the *Clarity* journey, the expressions "lights-on" and "that lights you up" convey the psycho-physical feeling of being passionate and energized, while "lights-off" refers to a feeling of being drained

Energy Meter: A means of calibrating how lights-on (energizing) or lights-off (draining) a person, place, or situation is.

Energy Pattern: An energy cluster in the personal energy field that manifests as a psychological complex or pattern of behavior.

Energy Scan: A very rapid assessment of approach or avoidance, used when encountering an unfamiliar person or environment.

High Noticing: Tuning in to energetic signals and vitality clues in yourself and your environment.

Law of Attraction: Energetic principle by which thoughts, words, and actions generate a force field of energy that draws an equal force field in return.

Lights-off: A low-energy, drained feeling that often appears as a dull or glazed look in the eyes.

Lights-on: An energized feeling that manifests as a look of radiance and vitality—an overall glow and a twinkle in the eye.

Monkey Mind: An inner voice that provides nonstop, self-critical, judgmental chatter.

Near Field: Your immediate surroundings—including home, family, office, automobile, neighborhood, and community—with which your personal energy field interacts continually.

Personal Field: The energetic space around you, extending an arm's length from your body, that receives information (feedback) from the near field.

Personal GPS: Inner guidance, or an instinctive knowing of what energizes and drains you.

Rapid Discovery: Speedy recognition of draining energy patterns.

Rapid Recovery: Speedy utilization of strategies to regain your energy.

Remote Field: The energy field most distant from you, over which you have little or no control.

Under the Line: A way of being that is energetically less effective, consisting of thoughts and behavior patterns that are energy-draining and problem-focused.

Vision: An image clearly seen in the imagination that creates a possibility for the future.

References and Bibliography

Briggs, John, and Peat, David. *Seven Lessons of Chaos—Spiritual Wisdom From the Science of Change*. New York: Harper Collins, 1999.

Buckingham, Marcus, and Coffman, Curt. *First, Break All The Rules*. New York: Simon & Schuster, 1999.

Campbell, Joseph. *The Power of Myth*. New York: Anchor Books, 1991.

Collinge, William. *Subtle Energy—Awakening to the Unseen Forces in Our Lives*. New York: Warner Books, 1998.

Collins, Jim. *Good to Great*. New York: Harper Collins, 2001.

Csikszentmihalyi, Mihaly. *Flow—The Psychology of Optimal Experience*. New York: Harper & Row, 1990.

Dyer, Dr. Wayne W. *The Power of Intention*. California: Hay House, 2004.

Emerald, David. *The Power of TED, The Empowerment Dynamic*. Washington: Polaris Publishing, 2006.

Hawkins, David. *Power vs. Force—The Hidden Determinates of Human Behavior*. California: Hay House, 1995.

Heerman, Barry. *Noble Purpose.* Virginia: QSU Publishing, 2004.

Heider, John. *The Tao of Leadership.* Georgia: Humanics New Age, 1985.

Hock, Dee. *The Birth of the Chaordic Age.* California: Berrett-Koehler, 1999.

Klein, Eric, and Izzo, John. *Awakening Corporate Soul.* Canada: Fairwinds Press, 1998.

Lapid-Bogda, Ginger. *Bringing Out the Best in Yourself at Work.* New York: McGraw Hill, 2004.

LeVoy, Gregg. *Callings—Finding and Following and Authentic Life.* New York: Harmony Books, 1997.

Lipton, Bruce. *The Biology of Belief.* California: Mountain of Love/Elite Books, 2005.

McTaggart, Lynne. *The Field—The Quest for the Secret Force of the Universe.* New York: Harper Collins, 2002.

Pink, Daniel. *A Whole New Mind; Moving from the Information Age to the Conceptual Age.* New York: Riverhead Books, 2005.

Roam, Dan. *The Back of the Napkin: Solving Problems and Selling Ideas with Pictures.* New York: Penguin Group, 2008.

Schwartz, Jeffrey, M.D., and Begley, Sharon. *The Mind & The Brain: Neuroplasicity and the Power of Mental Force.* New York: Regan Books, 2002.

Seligman, Martin. *Learned Optimism: How to Change Your Mind.* New York: Free Press, 1990.

Toms, Michael, and Justine Willis. *True Work—The Sacred Dimension of Earning a Living.* New York: Bell Tower, 1998.

Whyte, David. *Crossing the Unknown Sea, Work as a Pilgrimage of Identity.* New York: Riverhead Books, 2001.

Jaworski, Joseph. *Synchronicity, The Inner Path of Leadership.* California: Berrett-Koehler, 1996.

The Authors

Joining forces to bring their combined coaching expertise into this book, Cathy and Gary Hawk provide a proven process to transform the way people live and lead. As partners in Clarity International®, a boutique coaching and training firm, they specialize in creating energized workplaces through vision led business practices and focused actions. Clarity is a leader in the science of energy and its effects on life success.

Based on over 20 years of proven results with individuals, leaders and teams, the Clarity approach presents a visioning, leadership and communication model that is powerful, repeatable and sustainable. This innovative process heightens and clarifies innate skills of tuning in to energetic signals and vitality clues that are constantly being sent and received in everyone's life and work. Clarity clients focus on the energetic actions appropriate to their vision and clearly see what needs to be done to achieve it.

Founding Partner of Clarity International®, Cathy Hawk is a pioneer in the field of energy coaching. She has developed the innovative Clarity process that uses clearly observable data, such as camera imaging of the face and an interview process to awaken clients' energetic life force. This allows clients to see and follow their own energy with stunning clarity. As a result, they rapidly connect to their passion, look younger, feel energized, and quickly go into intentional action.

Since 1994, Cathy, along with Clarity-trained coaches, has inspired thousands of people from all walks of life to find and answer their callings, using energy as a primary life and work strategy. Drawing upon entrepreneurial expertise gathered from visioning and team building in her professional practice, she has coached visionary entrepreneurs and business owners throughout the U.S. and Canada, to create enlightened business practices.

Gary Hawk is Managing Partner of Clarity International®. Gary serves as an executive coach and mentor for CEOs, business owners and senior executives. He guides and challenges his clients in clarifying business and personal goals and in thinking through the ongoing means to attain them. The focus of his work is primarily on increasing the ability of each client to be an authentic leader of self and others, and developing a clarity of purpose and the methods to achieve it.

With over 40 years experience in both large and small businesses, Gary brings a rich business background to his mentoring relationships. Since 1994, Gary has also facilitated peer groups for CEOs and business owners. His peer groups provide a safe harbor for business owners to discuss the sensitive issues and challenges of leading and running a business.

To find out more about Clarity programs for
individuals, leaders and teams visit our website:

www.getclarity.com
or contact us at
info@getclarity.com

Bringing Clarity to You and Your Organization

There are several avenues to bring Clarity to individuals and organizations. Through our company, Clarity International®, we give keynote speeches, as well as, conduct workshops and retreats for individuals, leaders and teams. We can energize your team with a lights-on speech or deepen the experience with one- to four-day team retreats.

For individual leaders, several times each year, we offer our four-day retreat, *Get Clarity for Life and Work*™.

We know that the *Get Clarity Visioning and Operating System* will improve the personal leadership of every single person working in an organization. It creates a dynamic and trustworthy environment that fuels the generation of new ideas, new processes and new systems. Owners, managers and employees alike will be inspired to bring their whole selves to the office—body, mind and spirit.

Get Clarity workshops and retreats are all designed to give you the understanding and tools to transform the way you live and lead:

- Know what lights you up and what's next in your vision.

- Activate the deep energy that moves you to peak performance.

- Read the clues that ignite and renew your own passion and focus.

- Create a model of behavior and communication that delivers the vitality you want in your work and life.

- Energize more profitable relationships with your customers and employees.

- Remove judgment and criticism from your life and workplace.

- Avoid the commonly accepted workplace behaviors that actually inhibit everyone's performance.

For more information contact:
Clarity International®

www.getclarity.com
info@getclarity.com